"In twenty-seven concise chapt[...]
and challenges God's people to [...]
is Mark Jones at his best, combi[...] [...]theological breadth and depth with
his pastor's heart."

    Rosaria Butterfield, former professor of English, Syracuse University; author, *The Secret Thoughts of an Unlikely Convert*

"Most treatments of God's attributes are like vast mining operations that use massive theological machinery to plumb the depths of divine revelation. Mark Jones hands us the diamonds of God's perfections, already mined, cut, and polished, to enrich our souls immeasurably. Study this book, read it with your family, discuss it with your small group, teach it to your church class, and give it to your neighbor. This is a gem indeed!"

    Joel R. Beeke, president, Puritan Reformed Theological Seminary, Grand Rapids, Michigan

"Written in the tradition of J. I. Packer's *Knowing God,* Jones's work is an extremely helpful and needful primer on our great God and his all-beautiful character. Highly recommended as a tool for personal devotion or group study."

    Michael A. G. Haykin, professor of church history and biblical spirituality, The Southern Baptist Theological Seminary

"Mark Jones has offered the church a real gift in this book. His methodology is governed not only by the wise conviction that theology and application go together but also by the unwavering belief that to know God one must gaze upon his fullest self-revelation in Christ. In this light, he offers an accessible treatment of the divine attributes written not for academics but for faithful laity seeking to consider the wonder of God."

    Kelly M. Kapic, professor of theological studies, Covenant College, Lookout Mountain, Georgia

"Given the preoccupation in some evangelical circles with discovering the 'practical' outcome of every text, it is refreshing to have a book that enables us to simply contemplate and consider the nature and attributes of the God who is there. Never has evangelicalism been so confused or divided over that One who is the center and substance of our confessed faith. Never has there been such a clear need for every believer to sit down and examine and worship what has been revealed of the God who has saved us through his gospel."

    Liam Goligher, senior minister, Tenth Presbyterian Church, Philadelphia, Pennsylvania; author, *The Jesus Gospel*

"God is strangely absent from much contemporary Christ-centered preaching. This absence reflects not only a theological deficit but also a truncated view of Christ and the gospel. Mark Jones's devotional guide to the attributes of God is therefore a welcome contribution to the libraries of both pastor and layperson. *God Is* reliably unfolds the perfections of our triune God as revealed in Holy Scripture and confessed by the church, and it traces the various rays of God's perfections as they shine forth in the face of Jesus Christ."

> **Scott R. Swain,** president and James Woodrow Hassell Professor of Systematic Theology, Reformed Theological Seminary, Orlando, Florida

"While the Christ-centered characteristic of historic Reformed theology has been well documented in contemporary scholarship, Mark Jones is, to my knowledge, the only Reformed dogmatician of our day to have offered a thoroughly and explicitly Christocentric account of the divine attributes in ordinary language and pastorally applied this theology proper to the mundane spiritual life of the believer. If any contemporary book deserves the status of a sequel to Packer's *Knowing God* and the author's own *Knowing Christ*, this is it."

> **Shao Kai Tseng,** research professor, Department of Philosophy, Zhejiang University; author, *Karl Barth's Infralapsarian Theology*; contributor, *Oxford Handbook of Nineteenth-Century Christian Thought*

"Mark Jones continues to prove to be an especially reliable, pastoral guide in doctrine for the broader church. In the spirit of the great Puritan tradition—from which he so ably quotes—Jones once again melds depth and devotion, precision and passion, further proving J. I. Packer's axiom that 'true theology is for doxology.' Read *God Is* slowly, meditatively, with prayer, with others—and see if your thoughts of God are not greatly enlarged, reinvigorated, and warmed. It is a book I will suggest, give away, and return to myself for years to come."

> **Ryan Kelly,** pastor of preaching, Desert Springs Church, Albuquerque, New Mexico; council member, The Gospel Coalition

GOD IS

GOD IS

A Devotional Guide to
the Attributes of God

MARK JONES

WHEATON, ILLINOIS

God Is: A Devotional Guide to the Attributes of God

Copyright © 2017 by Mark Jones

Published by Crossway
   1300 Crescent Street
   Wheaton, Illinois 60187

Cover design: Jorge Canedo Estrada

First printing 2017

Reprinted with new cover 2020

Printed in the United States of America

Trade paperback ISBN: 978-1-4335-7423-8
ePub ISBN: 978-1-4335-5565-7
PDF ISBN: 978-1-4335-5563-3
Mobipocket ISBN: 978-1-4335-5564-0

Library of Congress Cataloging-in-Publication Data

Names: Jones, Mark, 1980– author.
Title: God is : a devotional guide to the attributes of God / Mark Jones.
Description: Wheaton : Crossway, 2017. | Includes bibliographical references and index.
Identifiers: LCCN 2017005040 (print) | LCCN 2017017633 (ebook) | ISBN 9781433555633 (pdf) | ISBN 9781433555640 (mobi) | ISBN 9781433555657 (epub) | ISBN 9781433555626 (hc)
Subjects: LCSH: God (Christianity)—Attributes. | Reformed Church—Doctrines.
Classification: LCC BT130 (ebook) | LCC BT130 .J66 2017 (print) | DDC 231/.4—dc23
LC record available at https://lccn.loc.gov/2017005040

Crossway is a publishing ministry of Good News Publishers.

VP		31	30	29	28	27	26	25	24	23	22	21
14	13	12	11	10	9	8	7	6	5	4	3	2

To Kevin and Patricia Jones, loving parents.
To Darren and Lara Jones, loving siblings.

Dogmatics, in each and all of its divisions and subdivisions, with every one of its questions and answers, with all its biblical and historical assertions, with the whole range of its formal and material considerations, examinations and condensations, can first and last, as a whole and in part, say nothing else but that God is.

Karl Barth, Church Dogmatics

How foolish are they who know not God! So many good things before their eyes, yet Him Who Is they fail to see.

Augustine, The Confessions

In Christ do we behold the wisdom, goodness, love, grace, mercy, and power of God, acting themselves in the . . . efficacious accomplishment of our redemption and salvation. This gives to us an unutterable lustre unto the native amiableness of the divine excellencies.

John Owen, Meditations and Discourses
on the Glory of Christ

CONTENTS

PREFACE

We believe that thou art a being than which nothing greater can be conceived.

Anselm, *Proslogion*

Whoever has seen God and has understood what he saw, has seen nothing.

Maximus the Confessor, *In Epistula Dionysii*

The majesty of God is too high to be scaled up to by mortals, who creep like worms on the earth.

John Calvin, *Institutes of the Christian Religion*

The true and living God is too much for us to bear, to handle, to conceive, to adore, to know, to trust, to understand, and to worship. The Incomprehensible One is simply too much for us in every conceivable way.

However, that the Son became flesh makes our human nature appear lovely to God. But he also makes God appear lovely to us.[1] Take away Christ, the God-man, and we are reprehensible to God and he to us. But in Christ, God is well pleased with us and we with him.

We look at God through Christ, who makes the attributes of God more delightful to us. As Thomas Watson says,

Christ clothed himself with our flesh, that the divine nature may be more pleasing to us. The human nature is a glass, through which we may see the love and wisdom and glory of God clearly represented to us. Through the lantern of Christ's humanity we may behold the light of the Deity. Christ being incarnate makes the sight of the Deity not formidable, but delightful to us.[2]

God so desires that we delight in him that he sent his Son into the world to be like us in every way yet without sin. I hope this book will help you, the reader, to that end: that in Christ, you should have exceeding delight in God. More importantly, I earnestly desire that in Christ, you should worship God, for the aim of any book on him is to bring us to such a place. And by that I mean not merely a place of private worship but also one of corporate worship, where our knowledge of God becomes clearer, better, and richer. As a result, in our worship as the church gathered, we shall know God better in order to worship God better.

At the age of twenty-seven, Jonathan Edwards preached a sermon in which he told his listeners that the "redeemed have all their objective good in God," because

God himself is the great good which they are brought to the possession and enjoyment of by redemption. He is the highest good, and the sum of all that good which Christ purchased. God is the inheritance of the saints; he is the portion of their souls. God is their wealth and treasure, their food, their life, their dwelling place, their ornament and diadem, and their everlasting honor and glory. They have none in heaven but God; he is the great good which the redeemed are received to at death, and which they are to rise to at the end of the world.[3]

We shall have God as our highest good only in Christ: "the sum of all that good which Christ purchased." We shall see and know

God but only in and through Christ. We shall have our reward from God but only from his Son.

Read on about your "great good," your "highest good," in the knowledge that God is indeed all these things to you in his Son, the Lord Jesus Christ, through the power of the Spirit of Christ (Rom. 8:9).

INTRODUCTION

Thus says the LORD: "Let not the wise man boast
in his wisdom, let not the mighty man boast in his
might, let not the rich man boast in his riches, but
let him who boasts boast in this, that he understands
and knows me, that I am the LORD who practices
steadfast love, justice, and righteousness in the earth.
For in these things I delight, declares the LORD."

Jeremiah 9:23–24

Let us know; let us press on to know the LORD.

Hosea 6:3

Knowing God

What can we say about God? What must we say about God?
These two questions are related but not identical. Even the Scriptures, the very words of God about himself, do not exhaust what
can be said about him. Indeed, as finite (limited) creatures, we
shall never be able to say everything about our infinite (unlimited)
God even in our perfect eternal state in heaven. We study God
not as he is in himself but as he is revealed in his Word. As James
Henley Thornwell says,

> God is at once known and unknown. In His transcendent Being,
> as absolute and infinite, though a necessary object of faith, He

15

cannot be an object of thought. We cannot represent Him to the understanding, nor think Him as He is in Himself. But in and through the finite He has given manifestations of His incomprehensible reality, which, though not sufficient to satisfy the demands of speculation, are amply adequate for all the ends of religion.[1]

For us today, these "manifestations" are summed up in God's Word, which dictates what we must say about him. We must affirm only what God has said about himself, which includes deducing truths about God by good and necessary consequence. In this life, we may not understand all that the Bible tells us about God, but we must aim to believe and communicate as much as we can about him. We must press on to know the Lord (Hos. 6:3), a difficult but rewarding task (Heb. 11:6). Worship without knowledge is idolatry.

All true theology depends on God. He is the principle on which our theology is constructed. As a personal, gracious God, he freely revealed himself to us. All other topics of theology (e.g., man, salvation, Christ) are held together by the doctrine of God. Hence, theology always remains to some degree the study of God.

The doctrine of God has fallen on hard times. Many are far more concerned about personal salvation than they are about God. Books on marriage abound, but books on the doctrine of God are few and far between. This is regrettable since nothing can ever really make sense to us in this life unless we have a good grasp of who God is.

To know God, we must love the Lord our God with all our heart, soul, strength, and mind (Luke 10:27). Our knowledge of God can never be limited to that which is merely grasped cognitively or academically. This book aims to help you love God with your mind but also with a great deal of strength, so that you can say with purity of heart (Matt. 5:8; 1 Tim. 1:5), "I know God." Eternal life is to know God (John 17:3). Charles Spurgeon, in a sermon on the immutability of God, says,

The most excellent study for expanding the soul, is the science of Christ, and him crucified, and the knowledge of the Godhead in the glorious Trinity. Nothing will so enlarge the intellect, nothing so magnify the whole soul of man, as a devout, earnest, continued investigation of the great subject of the Deity.[2]

Do you want your soul expanded? Listen to Spurgeon, who surely knew something about such expansion. But before you read on, note that he rightly connected the science of Christ with the knowledge of God as the way to make one spiritually healthy. The revelation of God shows Christ, who in turn discloses God. God created all things in order to glorify his Son (Col. 1:16), and the Son comes to reveal the Father (Matt. 11:25–27; John 17:5–6, 26). By the Spirit we enter this world of supernatural revelation, in which we can joyfully declare that through Christ we know God, which is eternal life.

Christ exists as the sacred repository of all truth. He manifests himself as the sum and center of God's revelation. He mediates not only through his saving work for the church but also by communicating between God and fallen humanity. His great aim on earth was to reveal God the Father (Matt. 13:35; John 1:18). In fact, Christ had a unique ability and capacity to give us knowledge of God (Prov. 8:22; John 1:3–4; 3:13; Heb. 1:2). What Christ received from the Father in terms of knowledge and grace he bestows freely on his bride. He does not wish to keep us ignorant. He delights to know God, and he desires the same joy for us.

Aims of the Book

Many of the greatest theologians in the church have written extensively on God. When I think of Augustine, Anselm, Abelard, and Aquinas—the "A Team"—I think of men who wrote majestically about a majestic God. Many after them have also written on the attributes of God. From what I can tell, the treatments by able, solidly orthodox theologians number in the hundreds. Beginning in the early church to the present day, we have been gifted with many excellent treatises on God, as well as many memorable sayings about God that have become entrenched in the annals of church history, such as Anselm's saying "We believe that thou art a being than which nothing greater can be conceived."[3]

Most of these treatments on the doctrine of God, however, are found in the middle of even larger works on dogmatic or systematic theology. And many of the best expositions of God's attributes come from the pens of men who wrote either in Latin or in an older English that at times makes for very difficult reading today.

In addition, the famous yet mammoth work *The Existence and Attributes of God* (1682) by the Puritan Stephen Charnock requires the sort of time and effort that very few have. As brilliant as the work remains, not only for its theological insight but also for its pastoral reflections, most people who honestly desire to know God better will never read his work from cover to cover.

As a result, my goal here is to provide a brief, simple, and clear book on the attributes of God that readers can (hopefully!) read from cover to cover. With a few exceptions, I avoid Latin, Greek, and Hebrew words or quotes as I diligently seek to make the doctrine of God simple (pardon the pun, and if you do not understand it, I hope you will by the end of the book).

Today, several theologians are defending various aspects of the doctrine of God in a way that continues the orthodox tradition handed down to us by the early church. Individuals such as Paul Helm, James Dolezal, Thomas Weinandy, and Stephen Duby, for example, are writing very good material on God's attributes, and I have very much appreciated their work. At the same time, their books can be rather heavy for the layperson who has read little in the doctrine of God. Because few things are as difficult as making the doctrine of God accessible, those with the ability, time, and desire should aim to be always instructing the church in the deep truths of the Christian faith with brevity and clarity (so Calvin). That is what I have attempted to do in this book.

I am also aiming to do something a little different from most treatments of the attributes of God. Not all books adequately apply the attributes of God to the Christian life. Perhaps the most notable example of a practical treatment of the doctrine of God remains J. I. Packer's monumental work *Knowing God*. His book has profoundly affected so many because it makes theology both easily accessible and eminently applicable. In this book I strive for such emphases and trust that the reader will find few things as practical for Christian living as studying God and his attributes. In each chapter I offer one or two selective (definitely not exhaustive!) points of practical application.

One further aspect of this study on the doctrine of God that I hope will distinguish it from others is its specific focus on Christ. Apart from Christ, the attributes of God remain meaningless to us. In Christ alone can we understand the true and living God, for Christ makes God's attributes beautiful and accessible to us as he rescues us from spiritual darkness and terror of God. Any so-called supernatural revelation of God apart from Christ is a lie, and any study of God's attributes is true only when it comes with a connection to his Son (Col. 1:16). We live and learn as Christians fixing our eyes on Jesus not just when we struggle with sin and temptation but also when we approach God in the Scriptures. To that end, no chapter on an attribute of God will omit reference to Christ, from whom alone comes an adequate understanding of such attributes.

In connection with this focus, the Puritan theologian Thomas Goodwin makes an important point:

> There is a glorious image of all God's attributes, which shines in the person of Christ . . . and in the works which Christ hath done for us, and in the fruits and benefits that redound thereby to us: or in the works of Christ . . . in us, now he is in heaven, leading us into communion with himself. And they all make a complete

image, and that more perfect, of the riches of God's glory: and this the gospel treats of.[4]

This study thus seeks to give you a sight of God and Christ and of how God's attributes affect your Christian living. To the degree that I can actually do this, as well as make complex theological concepts plain, I will regard myself a most blessed teacher, namely, one helping people know and love God in a better, clearer, and more informed way. The object of this book is to cultivate "in Spirit and truth" worshipers—the very kind God seeks (John 4:24).

A book of this size cannot say everything about God and does not deny a place for more detailed treatments on the attributes of God. I am by no means seeking to silence debates over the attributes in an age when orthodoxy has come under attack, even from within evangelicalism and the more broadly Calvinistic camp. Here I take much for granted that has been treated in greater detail elsewhere.

In addition, I have purposely chosen not to get too bogged down with classifying the attributes. Many are familiar with the incommunicable-communicable distinction. While that distinction has some value, I do not prefer it. When it comes to classifying God's attributes, I use the absolute-relative distinction. But in a book of this nature, those distinctions and discussions are unnecessary.

With these preliminaries in mind, along with my obvious dependence on Augustine, Anselm, Aquinas, and post-Reformation Reformed theologians such as Stephen Charnock, Edward Leigh, and John Owen, I hope that this book will help us know and enjoy God better.

Works on our great God should bring us joy, satisfaction, and a renewed appreciation for him. If this book does not do that, may it be cast aside and forgotten. Learn about and enjoy, I pray, the God you will spend eternity knowing and enjoying, through Christ Jesus our Lord. Amen.

1

GOD IS TRIUNE

The grace of the Lord Jesus Christ and the love of
God and the fellowship of the Holy Spirit be with
you all.

2 Corinthians 13:14

Doctrine

Before we discuss the divine attributes—for God's triunity is not
technically an "attribute" of God—we must keep in mind that
when we speak of God, we are speaking of the Christian God,
who is triune.

Christians are monotheists. We believe in the one true living
God (Deut. 6:4; 32:39; Isa. 44:8; 1 Cor. 8:6). But that does not
mean that all monotheists believe in the same God. When we
speak about God, we must relate his entire identity. Thus, while
attesting to the "singularity" and unity of the Godhead, we also
affirm just as strongly the triunity of the Godhead (Matt. 28:19).
The God who is one is at the same time three in persons. We embrace both "the One" and the "Splendor of the Three," echoing
Gregory of Nazianzus, who famously mused,

> No sooner do I conceive of the One than I am illumined by the
> Splendor of the Three; no sooner do I distinguish Them than I am

carried back to the One. When I think of any One of the Three I think of Him as the Whole, and my eyes are filled, and the greater part of what I am thinking of escapes me. I cannot grasp the greatness of That One so as to attribute a greater greatness to the Rest. When I contemplate the Three together, I see but one torch, and cannot divide or measure out the Undivided Light.[1]

In the Godhead, there are three persons: the Father, the Son, and the Holy Spirit. The Father is God, the Son is God, and the Holy Spirit is God. But God is one, and this one God is Father, Son, and Holy Spirit. We cannot deny this doctrine of the Trinity. We must hold to the unity of the divine essence (i.e., God's "whatness," or being) as well as the distinction of persons.

The Bible attributes deity to the Father, the Son, and the Holy Spirit:

1. The Father (Rom. 15:6; 2 Cor. 1:3–4; 1 Pet. 1:3)
2. The Son (Acts 20:28; Rom. 9:5; Titus 2:13)
3. The Holy Spirit (Ps. 95:3, 8–9 [cf. Heb. 3:7–11]; Acts 5:3–4)

Because the Scriptures ascribe divinity to three persons but also emphatically affirm that there is one God, Christian theologians in the early church spoke of what has become the Christian theological term *Trinity*. What is abhorrent to Jews and Muslims is most precious to Christians.

Whatever is said about the attributes of God is true of the Father, the Son, and the Holy Spirit. Therefore, if we say that God is omnipotent, we are saying that the three persons are all equally omnipotent. The same is true for all the divine attributes, which is why we use "essence-appropriate" language to speak of them. The same essence means the same power, wisdom, holiness, justice, goodness, and so forth, in the triune God. It also means the same will. Whatever God does toward himself or toward others is a result of his single divine will. Therefore, the persons never "submit" to each other in their eternal, necessary relations, because they share one will, not three distinct wills.

In addition to essence-appropriate language, we also use "persons-appropriate" language. So, for example, the Son, not the Father, became incarnate. The Father eternally begets the Son, but the Son does not eternally beget the Father. The Spirit proceeds from the Father and the Son, but the Father and the Son do not proceed from the Spirit. The doctrine of the Trinity means that there is no distinction of essence but rather a distinction of persons.

Throughout the history of the church, orthodox theologians have had to use extrabiblical language to analyze and discuss concepts found in the Bible. At various times over the centuries, heretics who only wanted to use biblical terminology criticized the orthodox for using the word *Trinity*. How did the orthodox respond?

According to John Owen, Christians must confess that God is one in "respect of his nature, substance, essence, Godhead, or divine being." At the same time, we affirm that this one God, "being Father, Son, and Holy Ghost, [subsists] in these three distinct persons or hypostases."[2] But in using this language, Owen employs words not found directly in the Bible.

Owen responds that to affirm the truth of the Trinity is to affirm a meaning or sense of such from the Scripture even when the words we use do not directly occur there. We envision the Trinity in our minds by thinking in terms of words such as *person*. To deny Christians this privilege is to make "brutes of ourselves." Thus, "in the declaration of the doctrine of the Trinity, we may lawfully, nay, we must necessarily, make use of other words, phrases and expressions, than what are literally and syllabically contained in the Scripture, but teach no other things."[3]

Importantly, if words other than those used in Scripture accurately convey its truth, then such words are "no less true and divine" than what was "principally revealed and directly expressed" in the Scriptures.[4] The true meaning of God's Word is divine truth.

Regarding the doctrine of the Trinity, then, Owen concludes that

> when the Scripture reveals the Father, Son, and Holy Ghost to be one God, seeing it necessarily and unavoidably follows thereon that they are one in essence . . . and three in their distinct subsistences . . . , this is no less of divine revelation than the first principle from whence these things follow.[5]

Here Owen is defending what the Westminster Confession of Faith calls "good and necessary consequence[s] . . . deduced from Scripture" (1.6). In other words, the doctrine of the Trinity is good in that it is biblically sound and necessary in that it is essential to believe as part of the whole counsel of God revealed in Scripture. The content of the phrase "God is one essence in three persons" is infallibly and inescapably true because it is deduced from the written Word of God. That is, we believe not only the *words* of God but also the *meaning* of God's words to us.

In sum, Francis Cheynell provides a helpful summary of the doctrine of the Trinity by affirming a number of the points mentioned above:

> We do believe that God is one, most singly and singularly one, and an only one: The unity of the Godhead is . . . a most singular unity. . . . All three Persons have one and the same single and infinite Godhead, and therefore must needs mutually subsist in one another, because they are all three one and the same infinite God[,] . . . united in their one nature, not confounded in their distinct subsistences; nay though their subsistence is in one another, yet their subsistences are distinct, but the nature most singularly the same.[6]

And the Westminster Confession of Faith gives us an excellent synopsis of the doctrine of the Trinity:

> In the unity of the Godhead there be three persons, of one substance, power, and eternity; God the Father, God the Son, and

God the Holy Ghost. The Father is of none, neither begotten, nor proceeding; the Son is eternally begotten of the Father; the Holy Ghost eternally proceeding from the Father and the Son. (2.3)

In Christ

In Christ, the triunity of God is revealed. The Trinitarian workings of God are stamped all over Jesus's life in the pages of the New Testament. While all outward works of God can be attributed to each of the three persons, certain outward works of God— depending on what they are—can be attributed more particularly to one of the three persons. In the incarnation of the Son of God, for example, we see a beautiful Trinitarian work.

The Father is not only the person who sent the Son of God to earth to redeem sinners but is also the master architect behind the type of body the Son assumed: "A body have you prepared for me" (Heb. 10:5). At the same time, the actual forming of the human nature of the Son through the flesh of the Virgin Mary was the work of the Holy Spirit (Luke 1:35). But the decision of taking into subsistence with himself a human nature was a prerogative that belonged to the Son, who must do all things freely and willingly. As Christ says, "I have come down from heaven" (John 6:38). In other words, while it is true that the Father sent the Son, the Son came willingly, apart from any coercion. The Son assumed a human nature.

Trinitarian emphases are literally everywhere in the ministry of Christ. Beginning with his baptism, whereby the Son hears the words of his Father and receives a special anointing of the Holy Spirit, we are faced with the workings of the triune God (Matt. 3:16–17). In his temptation, the Spirit thrusts Christ out into the wilderness (Mark 1:12), where he has to commit himself to believing the words of his Father. Would Christ believe what the Father had said at his baptism, or would he perform a miracle in order to prove his sonship (i.e., his messianic identity)? Even at his death, we see the Son of God offering himself up by the Spirit of God (Heb. 9:14) to God the Father (Luke 23:46). All this is to say that Christ's life was a revelation of the Trinitarian working of God.

Similarly, Paul brings out the Trinitarian focus of salvation in the first chapter of Ephesians. The works of God toward us are grounded in the Father's eternal love toward us in Christ, in which he elects us (Eph. 1:3–6). The Son becomes incarnate, and we are saved by his work for us in our stead (v. 7). And the Holy Spirit applies the work of Christ to us, endowing us with all spiritual blessings in Christ (vv. 13–14). In addition, the epistle of 1 Peter begins, "To those who are elect exiles of the Dispersion . . . , according to the foreknowledge of God the Father, in the sanctification of the Spirit, for obedience to Jesus Christ and for sprinkling with his blood . . ." (1 Pet. 1:1–2). Elected by the Father to be obedient, by the Spirit, to Jesus Christ in light of his sacrificial death—that is Peter's summary of salvation.

The Scriptures do not hide the constant Trinitarian workings of God. In the power of the Spirit, Christ reveals the Father. In the power of the Spirit, we love the Father through Christ. Indeed, the Christian life is meant to be lived with constant reference to the three persons. A truly Christian life will seek to be thoroughly Trinitarian in its theology and piety.

Application

Whether private or corporate, communion with God is Trinitarian communion. Thomas Goodwin speaks of how our communion can sometimes be with one person of the Trinity and sometimes with another:

> . . . sometimes with the Father, then with the Son, and then with the Holy Ghost; sometimes his heart is drawn out to consider the Father's love in choosing, and then the love of Christ in redeeming, and so again the love of the Holy Ghost, that searches the deep things of God, and reveals them to us, and takes all the pains with us; and so a man goes from one witness to another

distinctly. . . . We should never be satisfied till all three persons lie level in us, and all make their abode with us, and we sit as it were in the midst of them, while they all manifest their love unto us.[7]

We commune with the Father in love, thanking him and praising him for his eternal, free, life-changing, saving love (John 16:26–27; Rom. 5:5–6; 2 Cor. 13:14; 1 John 4:8–9). Owen expands on these terms, which are worthy of our reflection:

Eternal. It was fixed on us before the foundation of the world. Before we were, or had done the least good, then were his thoughts upon us. . . .

Free. He loves us because he will; there was, there is, nothing in us for which we should be beloved. . . .

Unchangeable. Though we change every day, yet his love changes not. . . .

Distinguishing. He has not thus loved all the world. . . . Why should he fix his love on us, and pass by millions from whom we differ not by nature?[8]

The Father loves us, though he is in himself all-sufficient. He is eternally and infinitely happy with his own glorious excellencies. He receives the love of the Son and the Spirit. Indeed, as Owen notes, "He had his Son, also, his eternal Wisdom, to rejoice and delight himself in from all eternity."[9] So we respond to this love with our own love for the Father, who has always loved us and who shows his love for us by giving us his Son to redeem us.

In relation to the Son, we commune with him in grace: "The grace of the Lord Jesus Christ and the love of God and the fellowship of the Holy Spirit be with you all" (2 Cor. 13:14). The one who is "full of grace and truth" (John 1:14), the Lord Jesus Christ, is the one who showers us with his grace: "For from his fullness we have all received, grace upon grace" (John 1:16). We enjoy Christ, the God-man, and we meditate not only on the grace given to us because of his work but also on the grace given to us because of who he is (i.e., his person). The greatness of Christ's person far excels even the benefits we receive from his work for us.

In the Lord's Supper, which is a Trinitarian activity, we receive grace from Christ in our communion with him. The gift of the body and blood is a gift given to us by the Father; the body and blood represent the now-resurrected Son; and we receive Christ into our hearts afresh through the work of the Spirit. The gospel is preached visibly to us, and by faith, in the power of the Spirit, we enter into communion with our Savior. He comes to us anew to comfort us with his promises and to stir up in us faith, hope, and love.

We also commune with the Spirit as he comforts, or helps, us: "And I will ask the Father, and he will give you another Helper, to be with you forever" (John 14:16). This verse carries a clearly Trinitarian accent: the Son asks the Father for the Spirit (i.e., the Helper) to be with his people.

We receive the promised Holy Spirit by asking in faith (Luke 11:13; John 7:37–39; Gal. 3:2, 14). There are many ways in which the Spirit helps or comforts believers. He glorifies Christ to us; he pours out the love of the Father and the grace of Christ into our hearts; he witnesses to us that we are children of the Father (Rom. 8:16); he produces faith and repentance in us; he generates in us "love, joy, peace, patience, kindness, goodness, faithfulness, gentleness, self-control" (Gal. 5:22–23).

The Spirit is also a guarantee for the believer, because God has "put his seal on us and given us his Spirit in our hearts as a guarantee" (2 Cor. 1:22; see also Eph. 1:13–14). He thus assures us that we will receive what God has promised to us, which is why the Spirit has been appropriately called "Comforter."

Finally, the Spirit brings us into communion with the Son and the Father (1 John 1:3). Apart from the Spirit, we would be as lifeless as the chairs we sit on. Owen writes,

All the consolations of the Holy Spirit consist in his acquainting us with, and communicating unto us, the love of the Father and the grace of the Son; nor is there any thing in the one or the other but he makes it a matter of consolation to us: so that, indeed, we have our communion with the Father in his love, and the Son in his grace, by the operation of the Holy Spirit.[10]

In our prayer life, then, we are also faced with our triune God. As children we come to our Father in the name of Christ by the power of the Spirit. We need all three persons in our life, for our life has the Trinity stamped all over it.

2

GOD IS SIMPLE

. . . he who is the blessed and only Sovereign, the
King of kings and Lord of lords, who alone has
immortality, who dwells in unapproachable light,
whom no one has ever seen or can see. To him be
honor and eternal dominion. Amen.

1 Timothy 6:15–16

Doctrine

If you asked most Christians, is God simple? they would likely
deny that to be the case. They might even be confused by the idea.
To call a person simple in today's common parlance is to insult
him or her. To call God simple is to glorify him. This observation
highlights that certain words have a rich theological pedigree that
is somewhat lost to us today.

The concept of divine simplicity is not easy to understand, but
we must prioritize this vital truth taught by theologians throughout church history. God is free from all composition. He is not
the sum of his parts. There is not one thing and another in God.
Rather, whatever is in God, God is. He is absolute, which means
that there are no distinctions within his being. As absolute, God
alone is the sufficient reason for his eternal existence.

God is not simply good but rather goodness itself. God is not merely powerful but rather omnipotence itself. More than that, when we speak of his attributes, we must keep in mind that because his essence remains undivided, his goodness is his power. Or, God's love is his power is his eternity is his immutability is his omniscience is his goodness, and so forth. In other words, there is technically no such thing as attributes (plural) but only God's simple, undivided essence.

Augustine asserts that every attribute is identical with God's essence and to that extent with every other attribute as well:

> For God to be is the same as to be strong or to be just or to be wise, and to be whatever else you may say of that simple multiplicity or that multiple simplicity, whereby his substance is signified. . . . That which is justice is also itself goodness, and that which is goodness is also itself blessedness.[1]

Or as Irenaeus observes,

> He is a simple, uncompounded Being, without diverse members, and altogether like, and equal to himself, since He is wholly understanding, and wholly spirit, and wholly thought, and wholly intelligence, and wholly reason, and wholly hearing, and wholly seeing, and wholly light, and the whole source of all that is good.[2]

God is eternally, unchangeably, infinitely, blessedly, powerfully good. As pure act—that is, a fully realized being in which there is no development—God has life in himself. In this, we rejoice that nothing can change who God is, because even the slightest alteration to his attributes would exterminate God.

Why is this important? The simplicity of God helps us to understand that perfect consistency exists in God's attributes. Mutability is absolutely inconsistent with simplicity, for God would not be God if he could be changed in any way. Stephen Charnock argues, "Where there is the greatest simplicity, there is the greatest unity; and where there is the greatest unity, there is the greatest power."[3] It is therefore incorrect to argue that God is the sum of all the divine attributes. Rather, the attributes are identical with the essence of God. Divine simplicity is absolutely essential for understanding the other divine attributes; indeed, they all depend on this concept.

The simplicity of God helps us to fully appreciate, as we should, the glorious promise found in Romans 8:28: "And we know that for those who love God all things work together for good, for those who are called according to his purpose." Because God is goodness, he can make this promise. But his goodness is also his power, so that he is powerfully good. Yet he is also wise, so he is powerfully good and powerfully wise. Add to this that God is unchangeably powerful and wise and good. Or, his power is his goodness is his wisdom is his unchangeability. We can therefore trust that all things are working together for our good because our God is wisdom, power, goodness, and immutability. All he does for us necessarily involves all these attributes.

When the Scriptures draw attention to one attribute, they invariably draw attention to another because, as noted above, it is hard to distinguish God's attributes in light of his simplicity. As soon as we talk about one, we are necessarily led to another. Consider David's praise in Psalm 145:8–9:

> The LORD is gracious and merciful,
>> slow to anger and abounding in steadfast love.
> The LORD is good to all,
>> and his mercy is over all that he has made.

As a simple being, God is graciousness is mercy is patience is love is goodness. He is all these things all the time with all attributes in perfect harmony. All the attributes of God must harmonize with one another in our conception of God, or else the God in our minds is not the true God.

God's Simplicity Revealed in Christ's Death

Christ reveals God to both men and angels. The angels receive their knowledge of God through the Son of God, who created them. Indeed, when the angels witnessed Christ's crucifixion on the cross, where the Father deserted him, they learned more about God and his attributes than in all the previous actions he had performed. As Thomas Boston declares,

> Again, the glory of one attribute is more seen in one work than in another: in some things there is more of His goodness, in other things more of His wisdom is seen, and in others more of His power. But in the work of redemption all His perfections and excellencies shine forth in their greatest glory.[4]

In Christ, all of God's attributes are manifested and glorified. Natural theology may give a person a dim knowledge of God's attributes, but in Christ, these attributes "sparkle" because they are revealed in redemption. Some even call Christ the "stage" on which God displays his attributes in their harmony for the world to witness. There is a profound sense in which the gospel reveals God in a way the law never could.

In the person and work of Jesus Christ, wisdom shines forth with a luster seen nowhere else in God's dealings with creation (Col. 2:3).[5] In this way, all that God is, Christ manifests as our Lord and Savior. For example, we observe God's wisdom through Christ's atoning death, which satisfies his justice, mercy, and love altogether. God punishes sin in Christ to satisfy his justice and holiness. God punishes sin in Christ to show us his mercy and love. God demonstrates his patience (i.e., divine forbearance) by not destroying sinners immediately (Rom. 3:25) because Christ's death was a future prospect for saints in the Old Testament. God is glorified in the way he saves sinners because it displays the harmony of his attributes. Thomas Goodwin speaks of redemption as God's "masterpiece, wherein he means to bring all his attributes upon the stage."[6]

A. W. Tozer notes, "When God justifies a sinner, everything in God is on the sinner's side. All the attributes of God are on the sinner's side. It isn't that mercy is pleading for the sinner and justice is trying to beat him to death. All of God does all that God does."[7] If God is for us, all of God, not a part of God, is for us. The infinite, eternal, unchangeable God who is goodness and wisdom himself is on our side (Rom. 8:31). So in the death of Christ, we see the simplicity of God revealed in the sense that all his attributes gloriously harmonize. We possess not a verse here or there but rather a glorious picture of God's simple undivided essence in the way he orchestrates the whole of our redemption, especially at the cross.

Application

Now what does this doctrine have to do with the Christian life? A great deal. In the person of Christ, we encounter a man who is not simple according to his humanity in the way that he is according to his divinity. But we have, in a manner of speaking, a sort of analogy in the Spirit-filled life of Christ. For example, he was a man filled with the Spirit (Luke 4:18–21). As the man of the Spirit par excellence, Christ's emotions were all kept in perfect harmony in the sense that he reacted perfectly to every situation. He knew when to weep and when to laugh (Eccles. 3:4–5), when to be righteously angry and when to be righteously merciful. He did good by keeping the law of the Lord with all his heart, soul, mind, and strength. In the way he observed the law and regulated his emotions, Christ provides us with a perfect example of the Spirit-filled life.

In Galatians 5, Paul contrasts the flesh and the Spirit (vv. 19–23). After describing the works of the flesh, he speaks of the fruit of the Spirit: "But the fruit of the Spirit is love, joy, peace, patience, kindness, goodness, faithfulness, gentleness, self-control; against such things there is no law" (vv. 22–23).

"Fruit" here is singular, which is absolutely vital for understanding Christian holiness. This means, then, that the various aspects of the fruit of the Spirit are interconnected. Hence, "love is patient and kind" (1 Cor. 13:4). Love is often love because it is patient kindness. In Galatians 5, Paul is saying that our love must be joyful love, patient love, peaceful love, faithful love, gentle love, and so forth. Our patience is joyful patience. In this way, when we manifest the fruit of the Spirit, we model in some sense God's simplicity. Consider the example of Moses in Hebrews 11:24–28:

> By faith Moses, when he was grown up, refused to be called the son of Pharaoh's daughter, choosing rather to be mistreated with the people of God than to enjoy the fleeting pleasures of sin [i.e., self-control]. He considered the reproach of Christ greater wealth than the treasures of Egypt, for he was looking to the reward [i.e., faithfulness]. By faith he left Egypt, not being afraid of the anger of the king, for he endured as seeing him who is invisible [i.e., patience]. By faith he kept the Passover and sprinkled the blood [i.e., peace], so that the Destroyer of the firstborn might not touch them [i.e., goodness].

Living in the power of the Spirit, Moses displays the fruit of the Spirit and all that this means. Those who have the Spirit cannot say that they excel in love but not in gentleness or patience. To have one grace is to have them all, because the Spirit is one, not many. The husband shows his love by being faithful and gentle in his love to his wife. The giver to God's work is the joyful giver.

Jonathan Edwards makes an important point in this regard:

> All the graces of Christianity always go together, so that where there is one, there are all; and when one is wanting, all are wanting. . . . The different graces of Christianity are in some respects implied in one another. They are not only always together, and do arise one from another; but one is, in some respects, implied in the very nature of another.[8]

For Edwards, the Spirit-filled life does not consist of parts. We love God and live obediently because of the Spirit who lives in us, enabling us to be not just loving or kind but loving, kind, joyful, peaceful, patient, good, faithful, gentle, and self-controlled. The Spirit-filled life represents an analogy of how God is all that he is in his simple, undivided essence.

3

GOD IS SPIRIT

God is spirit, and those who worship him must worship in spirit and truth.

John 4:24

Doctrine

We speak of God in a twofold sense: essentially and personally.
By referring to God *essentially*, we call attention to his divine
essence (i.e., substance). By speaking of him *personally*, we refer
to the triunity of God, who is Father, Son, and Holy Spirit. God
is spirit in terms of his essence; God is triune in terms of his
personhood.

What is God? In his conversation with the Samaritan woman
in John 4, Christ informs her, "God is spirit." In other words, God
is not corporeal or in possession of a body or material nature. He
is, as the hymn goes,

> Immortal, invisible, God only wise,
> In light inaccessible hid from our eyes,
> Most blessed, most glorious, the Ancient of Days,
> Almighty, victorious, thy great name we praise.[1]

When speaking of God essentially, we can understand him in
two different ways: (1) by way of affirmation (e.g., "God is good,"

or "God is spirit"), or (2) by way of negation (e.g., "God has no body," or "God cannot lie"). In the first instance, we ascribe to him whatever is excellent and reveals his glory. In the second instance, we separate or distinguish him from whatever is imperfect. Due to our human limitations, many theologians have suggested that the best way to describe God is by negation.

Readers will quickly notice, however, that the chapter titles in this book describe God by way of affirmation. Yet while each chapter ascribes to God whatever is excellent, each one also describes God by way of negation. That is, we want to separate from God whatever is imperfect. Thus, to speak of God as spirit affirms what he is and what he is not. For example, because he is spirit, we can affirm his infinity and independence, which by way of negation describes him as a being who is illimitable (i.e., without limit/end) and immutable (i.e., not capable of change). In terms of affirmation, we may say that God is omnipotent (i.e., all-powerful) or omniscient (i.e., all-knowing).

The Westminster Confession of Faith begins its chapter on God and the Trinity by affirming that "there is but one only, living, and true God, who is infinite in being and perfection, a most pure spirit, invisible, without body, parts" (2.1). We cannot see him with our eyes (1 Tim. 6:16). Thus, in the prologue to his Gospel, John tells his readers, "No one has ever seen God" (John 1:18). And Paul speaks of God as the "King of the ages, immortal, invisible" (1 Tim. 1:17). As a spirit, God is necessarily invisible.

Seeing God in Christ

The concept of the vision of God has a long and complicated history in the Christian church. How can God's people actually see God? Is it even possible? The answer is both yes and no. Indeed, God's children through the ages have longed to see him who is spirit. For example, Moses asked to see God's glory (Ex. 33:18), partly because he was God's representative to the people and partly because he wanted assurance of God's presence with him on Mount Sinai. The request to see God's glory was the same as asking to see him. After all, God replied, "You cannot see my face, for man shall not see me and live" (v. 20; see also v. 23). Paul certainly confirms this when he proclaims that God "dwells in unapproachable light, whom no one has ever seen or can see" (1 Tim. 6:16). Seeing God is not, as far as the Scriptures are concerned, the same thing as seeing a dog or seeing a soccer game.

Throughout the history of the church, theologians have spoken of the vision of God in a number of ways. First, to see God is to comprehend God. That remains utterly impossible for us as humans; finite creatures can never comprehend the infinite God. This matter is so important that we will return to it later.

Second, God "stoops" to our weakness by way of theophanies, whereby God, for the sake of revelation, makes himself visible. Over the course of church history, various theologians have objected to the idea that we cannot see God. These people have been called Anthropomorphites and have typically argued that the Scriptures are clear: God appeared to human beings. True, some people in the Old Testament saw partial revelations of him, but saying that they saw him "appear" (see Gen. 18:1) is not to say that they saw God in himself but to say that they saw him as he manifested himself for the sake of revelation.

Third, we "see God" in terms of his revelation, whereby he speaks to his creatures about who he is and what he does. As we read in Job,

Then Job answered the LORD and said:

"I know that you can do all things,
    and that no purpose of yours can be thwarted.
'Who is this that hides counsel without knowledge?'
Therefore I have uttered what I did not understand,
    things too wonderful for me, which I did not know.
'Hear, and I will speak;
    I will question you, and you make it known to me.'

> I had heard of you by the hearing of the ear,
>> but now my eye sees you;
> therefore I despise myself,
>> and repent in dust and ashes." (Job 42:1–6)

It is not just that Job now "understands" God better from the teachings in chapters 38–41 but that Job "sees" God because the Lord has directly confronted him in the thunderstorm (Job 38:1). We can thus speak of seeing God as a holy confrontation, whereby he takes the initiative to reveal himself to us, very often in the thunderstorms (or trials) of life.

When we have glorified bodies, we shall see God in the sense that we will possess a far greater understanding of his being than we are capable of here on earth in these jars of clay. Our happiness in this life and the one to come arises chiefly out of knowing God and all that that means for us as his children. Knowledge of the triune God, communicated to us through his Spirit-illumined Word, gives us a joy unspeakable.

Fourth, God enables his children to see him in the person of his Son. In the Upper Room Discourse in John's Gospel, Philip asks to see the Father (John 14:8). He claims that seeing the Father will make him content. But with a tender rebuke, Christ informs Philip, "Whoever has seen me has seen the Father. How can you say, 'Show us the Father'? Do you not believe that I am in the Father and the Father is in me? The words that I say to you I do not speak on my own authority, but the Father who dwells in me does his works" (vv. 9–10).

While it is impossible for us to see God, who is spirit, we truly "see" him in the face of Jesus Christ, who is "the image of the invisible God, the firstborn of all creation" (Col. 1:15). Thus, we see God in his Son, the God-man. We see the invisible God because of the visible man Christ Jesus. The desires of Moses and Philip are good desires. But they are only fulfilled through Christ, for it is impossible to see God as he "sees" himself.

Application

Because God is spirit, we who are both body and spirit (i.e., soul) stand in a most remarkable position. The omnipresent God dwells among and in his people. In his Upper Room Discourse, Christ promises that God will be with his people forever because the "Spirit of truth" will dwell in them (John 14:17).

The glory of the new covenant may be summarized thus: the Christ who is for us, in terms of his life, death, and resurrection, is also the Christ who is in us, because of the power of his ascended ministry in the heavenly places. God is spirit, but the Spirit of God dwells among his people based on the fact that Christ is in his Father: "In that day you will know that I am in my Father, and you in me, and I in you" (John 14:20). Hence, other parts of Scripture refer to the Holy Spirit as "the Spirit of Christ" or "the Spirit of Jesus" (Acts 16:7; Rom. 8:9; 1 Pet. 1:11). The apostle Paul nowhere better expresses this truth in his writings than when he prays for the Ephesians that "according to the riches of his glory he may grant you to be strengthened with power through his Spirit in your inner being, so that Christ may dwell in your hearts through faith" (Eph. 3:16–17). If God were not spirit, the realities expressed above—that Christ through his life-giving Spirit dwells in the hearts of his people—would be utterly impossible.

Returning to John 4:24, God as spirit carries implications for how we worship God. We must worship God in spirit and in truth. But what does that mean? When Christ speaks to the Samaritan woman, he is making a point that God is spirit. But of course, that is far from his only point. The Father, who gives the Spirit to his Son (Acts 2:33), entrusts Christ with the Spirit to create true worshipers, who will worship in the power of the Holy Spirit. The Holy Spirit, who brings glory to Christ, enables us to also bring glory to Christ in our own act of worship.

So John 4:24 describes not merely God's nature but also his relationship to us, his worshipers (see also 1 John 1:5, "God is light"). If we are not "in the Spirit" (that is, indwelt by the Spirit of Christ), we cannot worship. The Spirit enables us to join in heavenly worship, for there is no proper worship that is not heavenly.

Worship in the Spirit is also worship in the truth. So as soon as we conceive of worship in the Spirit, we are also drawing our minds to the truth that God is Father, Son, and Holy Spirit. Worship must be Trinitarian if it is spiritual worship. Trinitarian worship is also Christ-centered worship, for the Spirit supernaturally enables us to call on Christ's name, glorify his name, and rejoice in his name.

The truth is, then, that God is spirit. But far from being simply a metaphysical declaration about God's essence, it gets us to the heart of the Christian faith: that God dwells in the hearts of his people, enabling them to offer worship that is acceptable. "God is spirit, and those who worship him must worship in spirit and truth" (John 4:24). If our worship is not saturated with truth, then we can hardly claim to be worshiping God in the Spirit, for the Spirit works according to the truth.

Thus, the more our human words replace God's words in corporate worship, the more we are corporately quenching the Holy Spirit. That is not to say that we cannot use human words, such as in our hymn singing. But certainly the Bible should be read corporately, and our prayers should be suffused with Scripture. Exclusive psalmody is not, in my mind, biblically demanded, but excluding the Psalms altogether from our singing is a greater crime than singing only the Psalms. After all, the Psalms give us perhaps the grandest view of God in all his Word, which drives us back again to the Spirit-filled, Word-informed worship appropriate to the nature of our God.

4

GOD IS INFINITE

Can you find out the deep things of God?
> Can you find out the limit of the Almighty?
It is higher than heaven—what can you do?
> Deeper than Sheol—what can you know?
Its measure is longer than the earth
> and broader than the sea.

Job 11:7–9

Doctrine

The infinity of God is sort of like a "meta-attribute," such as simplicity, in the sense that it qualifies all the other attributes. [Infinity means that there is no limit to God's perfections.]

Stephen Charnock helps us as we think about this concept:

> Whatever God is, he is infinitely so. . . . Conceive of him as excellent, without any imperfection; a Spirit without parts; great without quantity; perfect without quality; everywhere without place; powerful without members; understanding without ignorance; wise without reasoning; light without darkness; infinitely more excelling the beauty of all creatures. . . . And when you have risen to the highest, conceive him yet infinitely above all you can conceive of spirit, and acknowledge the infirmity of your own

minds. And whatsoever conception comes into your minds, say, "This is not God; God is more than this."[1]

In the seventh century, Maximus the Confessor said, "Whoever has seen God and has understood what he saw, has seen nothing."[2] Indeed, we cannot grasp the Infinite One. Many theologians, such as John Flavel, have spoken of infinity in relation to three related but different aspects:

1. Respecting the perfection of his essence, "his wisdom, power, and holiness, exceed all measures and limits."
2. Respecting time and place (i.e., eternity and omnipresence), "no time can measure him."
3. Respecting his incomprehensibility, finite creatures cannot comprehend the infinite God.[3]

Bavinck provides another way of understanding God's infinity: "When applied to time, God's immutability is called eternity; when applied to space, it is called omnipresence."[4] Infinity helps us to understand how immutability and eternity coincide or how immutability and omnipresence relate.

When we consider God's attributes, we must always consider them as infinite. His infinity is a positive concept, so that we must say that his attributes are intensively and qualitatively infinite. God's infinity is the highest sense of perfection. "Not yet finished" (or "indefinite") is an improper way to understand *infinity* with regard to God. Rather, without bounds or limits or degrees, God knows infinitely (Isa. 40:28) and is a sphere whose center is everywhere and circumference nowhere. He is as present in our midst as he is farthest from us in the universe. Yet while he is present in one place, he is never confined to any place.

The psalmist explicitly acknowledges God's infinity: "Great is our Lord, and abundant in power; his understanding is beyond measure" (Ps. 147:5). God's understanding exists without measure. The psalmist here combines one attribute with another, as he does elsewhere. God is great, because he is abundant in power (omnipotent) and measureless (infinite) in his understanding (omniscience).

Because God is eternal and omnipotent, nothing can limit him or be too hard for him: "Behold, I am the Lord, the God of all flesh. Is anything too hard for me?" (Jer. 32:27). He is the eternal, independent, powerful God who determines all things. He is perfection, so that nothing extends beyond him. God's infinity consists not in "indefiniteness" or "potentiality" but in the perfection of his attributes. God is fully actualized potentiality. In other words, he cannot "become" anything; he always has and always will be what he alone is: a fully actualized being who needs nothing and possesses everything.

[Affirming God's infinity implies his incomprehensibility.] We can never know God as he knows himself, for the finite cannot comprehend the infinite. We possess a bounded understanding, because we are creatures. God has a boundless understanding as the infinite, eternal God. We could sooner fit the oceans of the world in a teacup than understand God. Our grasp of God compared with God's actual being is like a dim light compared with the vast radiance of the sun. We can say with certainty that what we know about God can never be full but only adequate (i.e., saving) knowledge, which can always increase.

The Worth of Christ

The Son of God assumed a human nature in order to perform the work of Mediator on behalf of fallen sinners. The efficacy of his work depends on the worth of his person. It is "the dignity of the person that dignifies the work," argues Thomas Goodwin.[5] He adds, "As all the Godhead in all his fullness is said to dwell in him and his person, so all the whole worth that the substantial excellency of the person can translate is in like manner stamped upon all his actions."[6]

Many Christians and theologians maintain that we should not say that the second person of the Trinity died, because that would constitute a mutation within the very being of God. They are uncomfortable saying that God died on the cross. Instead, they prefer to say that Christ (the God-man) died on the cross in his humanity while inseparably united to his divinity, which could not die. While we can sympathize with the discomfort for insinuating that God died, this view essentially limits the atonement to Christ's humanity. This in turn has ramifications for the infinite worth of Christ's death for multitudes of sinners, as we shall see.

We must keep in mind the distinction between asserting something in essence-appropriate and persons-appropriate language. We could say, then, that in relation to their persons, the Son and the Spirit are from the Father, but in relation to their essence they are self-existent.[7] Theologians have by and large used this distinction to maintain a unity of essence but also affirm a relational order in terms of the three persons. The Father begets the Son, not the other way around. Therefore, persons-appropriate language explains why we can say that the Father did not die on the cross but the Son did.

If we affirm, as we should, that God purchased the church with his blood (Acts 20:28), we are saying that he purchased the church with his death. We should have freedom (and the theological tools) to preach, pray, or sing what the Scriptures explicitly teach. The mystery and glory of the gospel demand that we say things that can possibly be misunderstood (e.g., justification by faith alone and the Roman Catholic response to that blessed doctrine).

Some might worry that this means that the deity suffered, so they would then shrink back from affirming that the Son of God (the second person) died on the cross. But we can say that God the Son died because of the *communication of properties*, a theological term that, according to Francis Turretin, means that "the person indeed claims for itself the properties of both natures, but one nature does not claim for itself the properties of the other, which belong to the person."[8] The Westminster Confession of Faith summarizes this doctrine quite well: "Christ, in the work of mediation, acts according to both natures, by each nature doing that which is proper to itself; yet, by reason of the unity of the person, that which is proper to one nature is sometimes in Scripture attributed to the person denominated by the other nature" (8.7). Hence, we can predicate death or hunger to the person of the Son because of the communication of properties, even though only the human nature can experience death or hunger.

It follows, then, that we do not say that God suffered on the cross in an abstract or general way as the divine essence. However, when we speak of God the Son dying and shedding his blood (in line with Acts 20:28), we are speaking about the concrete person of Christ, the God-man.

We have to say that the person, not a nature, died. Jesus, the God-man, died on the cross. It was not simply the humanity of the God-man that died, for that would divide his person. The current status of Jesus helps us to understand this idea. We can rightly say that the person seated at the right hand of God the Father is the second person of the Trinity. However, we would not claim that this person is only the divine nature of Jesus (leaving us with a vestige of Christ) since his human nature does not share in the divine essence of the Godhead. Rather, because of the communication of properties, we rightly state that Jesus, the God-man, is the second person of the Trinity. Similarly, when Thomas looked on the resurrected Christ, he cried out, "My Lord and my God!" (John 20:28). He did not qualify himself by stating, "Now, of course, I do not mean God in your humanity but only God in your divinity, even though my current amazement stems from seeing you in the flesh." He simply looked on Jesus and called him God.

So we must avoid implying that the atonement was made by the human nature of Christ. Natures do nothing in the abstract. We are concerned about the concrete person in all of Christ's acts of mediation: the Son did this, or the Son did that. Christ the person atoned for sin because the atonement needed to be infinite in value. After all, one person died for millions and millions of persons. This is possible because God accepts the sacrifice of his Son; as Goodwin notes, "For as the offence is against an infinite glorious God, so the holy works are wrought by one as Infinite."[9]

We cannot afford, then, to be tentative about the infinity of God. Our salvation rests on the fact that the Infinite One became man to die in the place of sinners, who transgressed against an infinitely holy God, who demanded justice if ever he would forgive us. Only the payment of his infinitely glorious Son would suffice.

In our finitude, we are unable to comprehend an infinite God, yet the gospel enables us to see so much more of God than would otherwise have been possible. As Thomas Goodwin notes,

> The "back-parts" of God, which we call his attributes, his power, wisdom, truth, justice, which God calls his glory to Moses . . . and which we cannot see and live: these are infinitely more really and substantially . . . set forth to us, by what we know of Christ as a redeemer in the gospel; and do infinitely transcend whatever of them either was, or could have been expressed in millions of several worlds, filled all of them with several sorts of intelligent creatures, such as angels and men.[10]

Thus, in the gospel not only are we saved by the infinite worth of Christ's sacrifice, but also in his death we have "infinitely" more knowledge of God than we could have had without the supernatural revelation of Christ.

Application

The doctrine of God's infinity gives us great joy because it assures us that our sins are forgiven, due to the infinite worth of Christ's sacrifice. Additionally, we can rejoice that we as finite creatures can never comprehend the infinite. Far from being a problem, this doctrine is a delight, for we shall one day be given glorious resurrected bodies. As Paul says, "Just as we have borne the image of the man of dust, we shall also bear the image of the man of heaven" (1 Cor. 15:49).

In this exalted state, we will be able to perfectly apply our minds to the knowledge of God and Christ by means of the Holy Spirit illuminating our spiritual and intellectual faculties. We shall spend an eternity knowing God, because he is the infinite God. Yet even for all eternity, we shall never fully comprehend God. Still, this impossibility remains our delight insofar as we have so much to look forward to in what awaits us. By *knowing God*, I do not mean merely coming to a greater awareness of who he is but also coming to a greater awareness of all that he has done and will continue to do for us, including our understanding of his attributes displayed in the new creation. We all, for example, shall be true scientists of the highest order.

But we should always remember our established place as creatures. We serve an infinite God, and our praises in this life come so very short of what is due to him. But he accepts our praises, despite our weaknesses. The Infinite One stoops and stoops and stoops in order to raise us to places that are undeserved. Our union with the infinite Son of God puts us in the most privileged place possible for a human being—far more privileged than Adam's place in the garden. We belong to an infinite God who will satisfy us forever because he alone is in the position to pour out everlasting blessings on his creatures. As Matthew Mead puts it,

> Alas! it is an infinite righteousness that must satisfy for our sins, for it is an infinite God that is offended by us. If ever your sin be pardoned, it is infinite mercy that must pardon it; if ever you be reconciled to God, it is infinite merit must do it; if ever your heart be changed, and your soul renewed, it is infinite power must effect it; and if ever your soul escape hell, and be saved at last, it is infinite grace must save it.[11]

5

GOD IS ETERNAL

Have you not known? Have you not heard?
The LORD is the everlasting God,
   the Creator of the ends of the earth.
He does not faint or grow weary;
   his understanding is unsearchable.

Isaiah 40:28

Doctrine

God is the everlasting God. Or to put it another way, God is eternal: "The eternal God is your dwelling place, and underneath are the everlasting arms" (Deut. 33:27). But as soon as we make this statement, we run into a serious problem. We simply cannot conceive of or express God's eternity because we are beings who have not always existed but were created by a God who has always been and will always be. Our minds are puzzled by such a concept: "Behold, God is great, and we know him not; the number of his years is unsearchable" (Job 36:26). In the words of Stephen Charnock, "If man compares himself with other creatures, he may be too sensible of his greatness; but if he compares himself with God, he cannot but be sensible of his baseness."[1]

What do we mean when we say that God is eternal? First, his eternality is unlike the eternal state experienced by humans or angels, all of whom were created in time. Time has a beginning with succession of moments, but God has no beginning, succession of moments, or ending (Gen. 1:1; Job 36:26; Ps. 90:2). God's eternality speaks of his timeless and unchangeable (yet not static) nature. As theologians of the past have argued, the statement "Time began with the creature" rings truer than "The creature began with time."

God has no beginning. Think about that. He has always existed. Nothing brought him into being. It boggles the mind. He is called the "Ancient of Days" (Dan. 7:9), but even this phrase remains an "improper" way of speaking about God's eternality, for he does not get old; he is not ancient or young. Rather, the phrase "Ancient of Days" suits our limited understanding by pressing home to us that God contains in himself all times and ages.

God has no ending (Ps. 9:7; Rev. 4:9–10). Just as no other being can give God life, so no other being can take his life away from him. If Christ could say in John 10:18, "No one takes [my life] from me, but I lay it down of my own accord," how much more may we say that no one takes God's life away from him?

God has no succession of moments. God's eternality cannot be abstracted from his other attributes, such as immutability (i.e., he cannot change) or omniscience (i.e., he is all-knowing). God comprehends all things at once. He does not increase in knowledge and wisdom. He sees all things that have ever been or shall ever be at once, which we may call an "eternal present." Louis Berkhof speaks of such in his observation that God is above all time "and therefore not subject to its limitations. [For Him there is only an eternal present, and no past or future."]² Charnock similarly notes that since eternity is "contrary to time," it is "a permanent and immutable state," and as "immensity is the diffusion of [God's] essence, so eternity is the duration of his essence. . . . His duration is as endless as his essence is boundless."³

To illustrate the idea of the eternal present, think of watching a baseball game. We watch a live game in a succession of moments. We do not infallibly know each detail of the game before it happens. We wait for the game to unfold before our eyes. In other words, the ninth inning comes after the first eight innings. But God does not watch baseball games the way we do. God sees every event in the game at once. He sees the ninth inning at the same time as he sees the first inning. Yet God does not conflate the ninth inning with the first inning. Now extrapolate that to world history: God can infallibly predict future events because he sees the future as well as he sees the past. He has declared the end from the beginning (Isa. 46:9–11).

Anselm beautifully captures all these ideas in the following:

> Through your eternity you were, you are, and you will be. And since being past is different from being future, and being present is different from being past and from being future, how does your eternity exist always as a whole? Does none of your eternity pass by so that it no longer is, and is none of it going to become what, so to speak, it not yet is? Then, in no case were you yesterday or will you be tomorrow; instead, yesterday, today, and tomorrow, you are. Or better, you simply are—existing beyond all time. You do not exist yesterday or today or tomorrow; for yesterday, today, and tomorrow are nothing other than temporal distinctions. Now, although without you nothing can exist, you are not in space or time but all things are in you. For you are not contained by anything but rather you contain all things.[4]

Because we are temporal creatures, grasping eternity lies beyond us. But we can reflect on God's eternality and can marvel at the language we are privileged to use in describing our eternal God.

Christ's Gift of Eternal Life

The Son who is "before all things" (Col. 1:17), and thus the eternal God, entered time and became subject to the conditions of time. According to his humanity, Christ was subject to extrinsic time and intrinsic time. By extrinsic time, Christ, who made the heavens (e.g., the planets, the stars), measured their motion. By intrinsic time, he grew up and could look forward to the Sabbath or a good meal (Luke 19:5). He had a past, present, and future. Because his humanity was created, like ours in every way except without sin, he possessed intrinsic time, which is a characteristic of all created things.

[The eternal Son of God—in need of nothing, knowing all things, possessing all things—entered time so that we might have eternal life (John 3:36). He willingly subjected himself to all the realities of time (e.g., living by faith and in hope) in order to give us the gift of eternal life.]

We note something of time and eternity in the person of Christ in Psalm 90. The psalmist sets forth his eternity in verse 2: "Before the mountains were brought forth, or ever you had formed the earth and the world, from everlasting to everlasting you are God." For Christ, however, he was also taught to number his days (v. 12). He passed away under his Father's wrath (v. 9). As the exalted Messiah, Christ's days have no end (Ps. 102:27; Heb. 1:12). And those who are "in Christ" will share in this reality.

But does that mean we are eternal as God is eternal? No. We possess *aeviternity*, which has a beginning but no ending. This word was used both by Reformed theologians and by medieval scholastics (e.g., Bonaventure). Angels and humans possess aeviternity. God's eternality includes his vast omniscience; our eternal state means growing in the knowledge of God forever but never knowing all as only God can. Still, only an eternal God can grant "eternal" life.

Application[5]

The eternality of God has many important implications for the Christian life, including how we should think of the eternal destinies of all humans.

When we speak of grace, hell, heaven, and other doctrines, we must speak not in generalities but in specifics, as do the Scriptures, which highlight good and necessary consequences (see Matt. 22:32). For example, a preacher may ineffectively reference the horrors of hell if he fails to explain why hell will be so horrible and heaven so happy. Even the popular idea that hell is "separation from God" is a misleading and inaccurate description of the eternal torment awaiting the damned. In fact, a God-hating sinner without a Mediator will live for eternity in the presence of a holy, righteous, and powerful God. The wicked in hell, though, will have no desire for union with God, which is a chief mark of love. Thus, while in the presence of God, they will have no desire to be with God.

Christ spoke on hell more than anyone else in the Bible. But he did not merely talk about hell; rather, he described hell concretely (Matt. 10:28). For example, consider the language of Luke 3:17, which ends by describing hell as an "unquenchable fire." Elsewhere, we encounter hell as a "fiery furnace" with the presence of "weeping and gnashing of teeth" (Matt. 13:42). Hell confronts us as a "lake of fire" (Rev. 19:20), an "eternal fire" (Jude 7), "outer darkness" (Matt. 22:13), blackness of darkness forever (Jude 13), and a place where "their worm does not die and the fire is not quenched" (Mark 9:48). Hell is eternal, that is, forever.

We can contrast the torments of hell with the joys of heaven from the perspective of time. In doing this, we can better understand the glories of heaven and the terrors of hell. True, hell is a punishment so great and heaven a reward so wonderful that we can comprehend neither properly in this life. Christians will receive eternal life (John 5:24), and those who do not love the Lord Jesus with an undying love will receive eternal death (1 Cor. 16:22). But how do we seek to join with Paul, for example, in persuading men because of the terrors of the Lord (2 Cor. 5:11) as we reflect on time in eternity? One way is for preachers to remind their hearers that in hell it will feel as though there is only time—*slow* time. In this world, when we suffer, time seems to stand still. Even waiting in traffic or in a doctor's office, time crawls. We become more sensitive to the seconds. This happens when listening to poor sermons too.

However, those in heaven will experience something entirely different because they resemble Christ, possessing joy unspeakable. Time flies when you're "having fun." Imagine how time will seem to evaporate in heaven because of the joy we will experience. Or consider the time spent talking to a relentless telephone salesman compared with getting to know your future wife or husband. In the former, like hell, a second feels like a year. In the latter, like heaven, a year feels like a second.

We can note two related observations:

1. In heaven, our joy can only increase, not decrease. Knowing that our joy will grow heightens the joy experienced at that moment. In this life, we can feel sadness in knowing that a current joy will come to an end (e.g., my vacation of a lifetime ends tomorrow). Not so in heaven. There our joys will never end, which will therefore elicit even greater joy in each successive moment.

2. For those consigned to hell, their despair will also increase, not decrease. They will never again experience the relief we get in this life of knowing that a difficulty will soon pass (e.g., the nurse who anticipates the end of a stressful twelve-hour shift). As the creature in hell realizes more and more that he or she will suffer forever, the despair of eternal judgment can only increase. Hope has utterly vanished. In our sufferings here on earth, we always have the promises of God to look to (Rom. 8:18, 28–30). But those in hell have no promises and thus no hope, which only increases despair.

According to Thomas Goodwin, in hell the wicked will despair, for the "wretched soul in hell . . . finds that it shall not outlive that misery, nor yet can it find one space or moment of time of freedom and intermission, having for ever to do with him who is the living

God."[6] The wicked will be miserable, because God's wrath never ceases for them. For that reason, the wicked will exist in total dread, tormented by what they experience not just in the present moment but also forever.

The only response of the creature in hell will be to blaspheme God since there will be no goodness in them with which to praise God. As a result, there can be no end to the sinner's punishment. God's eternality, coupled with the sinner's perpetual blasphemy against him, demands an eternal place of torment. The concept of ever-increasing eternal despair for damned sinners continually blaspheming God gives us every reason to persuade men, women, and children to flee to the One who endured hellish despair on the cross for others (2 Cor. 5:11–21).

If you really believe in the cross of Christ, then you must accept the reality of hell. If you believe that hell exists, then you are beyond thankful that there was a cross for Christ.

6

GOD IS UNCHANGEABLE

They will perish, but you will remain;
    they will all wear out like a garment.
You will change them like a robe, and they will
        pass away,
    but you are the same, and your years have
        no end.
The children of your servants shall dwell secure;
    their offspring shall be established before you.
Psalm 102:26–28

Doctrine

As we explore each of the attributes of God, we quickly realize that one attribute necessarily explains another. For example, God's eternality has obvious implications for how we understand his immutability or unchangeable nature. Herman Bavinck helpfully overlaps these two perfections (along with others): "Every change is foreign to God. In him there is no change in time, for he is eternal; nor in location, for he is omnipresent; nor in essence, for he is pure being."[1]

The Scriptures frequently refer to God's unchangeable nature:

"For I the LORD do not change" (Mal. 3:6; see also Isa. 14:27; 41:4). Many of these passages refer to his ethical immutability, which denotes his covenant faithfulness to his promises. Such moral unchangeability arises out of God's ontological immutability, which refers to the fact that he can never change in his being or essence. If God could change, we could never be certain of his promises. Hence, his ontological immutability provides the foundation for his unchangeable promises toward us in Christ.

God is what he always was and will be (James 1:17). Because of his simplicity, his eternality demands his immutability. Eternity speaks about the duration of a state, whereas immutability is the state itself. Immutability in God means not only that he does not change but also that he cannot change (Ps. 102:26). God's immutability provides his people with a great deal of comfort and stability. So, for example, when theologians have historically argued that God is immutable, they have called attention to his unchangeable goodness, love, holiness, power, and wisdom. Do we want a God whose love may change? Do we want a God whose holiness can change? Do we want a God whose power may change? What a blessing to affirm God's immutability.

If we apply God's eternality and immutability to his knowledge, then we have to say that God knows all things at once. Immutability precludes change in God's knowledge. In addition, because he is spirit, God is not subject to mutations that belong to those with bodily natures.

The Puritan Thomas Vincent aptly summarizes the several ways that we are to understand how God is unchangeable:

1. God is unchangeable in regard to his nature and essence (Ps. 102:25–27).
2. God is unchangeable in regard to his counsel and purpose (Isa. 46:10).
3. God is unchangeable in regard to his love and special favors (Rom. 11:29; James 1:17).[2]

God's immutability regarding his promises and purposes provides great comfort: "God is not man, that he should lie, or a son of man, that he should change his mind. Has he said, and will he not do it? Or has he spoken, and will he not fulfill it?" (Num. 23:19). His promise that all things work together for the good of those who love God (Rom. 8:28) would be jeopardized if he could change in his purposes toward us. Indeed, God's immutable promises and purposes toward Christ afforded assurance even for him (e.g., John 17), but that assurance would have been lost if God could change.

If, however, God cannot change in his being or knowledge, what do we make of the biblical passages that speak of him "repenting"? Historically, Reformed orthodox theologians have argued that God repents not properly but only relatively. In a humanlike (anthropomorphic) expression of repentance, he freely and graciously accommodates himself to the weakness and finitude of humans, who are limited in their understanding of him. God does not truly repent, for such would imply sin or at least the need to change his mind about some previous course of action, which would in turn contradict his infallible knowledge of all things, as if something happened unexpectedly or took him by surprise.

In other words, since finite creatures cannot comprehend the infinite God, he will sometimes clothe himself with our nature in certain scriptural expressions, so that "we may apprehend him as we are able, and by an inspection into ourselves, learn something of the nature of God."[3] So when Genesis 6:6 says that God repented that he had made man, that teaches us something about God's hatred of sin. Such anthropomorphic expressions "ascribe the perfection we conceive in them to God, and lay the imperfection at the door of the creature."[4]

In summary, God's attribute of immutability is too clear and too vital to affirm hesitantly or with reservation. If his essence can be changed, only a being more powerful than him can do so. The

Scripture texts that imply God's change of mind are overwhelmed by those clearly teaching his immutable being and knowledge. Reformed orthodox theologians have reconciled the apparent contradictions in these passages to set forth a consistent doctrine of immutability. They have thus denied that God repents *properly* and have instead affirmed that he repents *relatively*, a term that reflects the language of accommodation. In this way, men and women are driven to see in these statements both their own imperfections and the perfections of God.

The Unchangeable Changed

In Christ, we behold one who is both unchangeable and changeable. In short, the unchangeable Son of God took on changeable humanity (i.e., mutability) in order that we (mutable humans) might enter a state of immutability.

Hebrews 1:10–12 cites Psalm 102:25–27 to establish the Son's superiority to the angels by showing the eternality and immutability of Jesus: "They will perish, but you remain. . . . [Y]ou are the same, and your years will have no end" (Heb. 1:11–12). Christ's divine status as Israel's King gives his subjects great assurance of his superiority to all angelic beings. This same Jesus, the writer of Hebrews says, "is the same yesterday and today and forever" (Heb. 13:8), the eternal and unchangeable One (see Heb. 1:8). But this eternal "sameness" attests not simply to his being but also to his priesthood (Heb. 5:6; 6:20; 7:17, 21, 28). And through this eternal ministry, he has accomplished an eternal salvation (Heb. 5:9; 7:24–25; 9:12) for his people (Heb. 9:15).

Leaders, prophets, teachers, and ministers come and go in the church, but Jesus Christ, by virtue of his being and office as priest, always ministers to his people without changing in his attitude and purposes toward them. Christ's person (i.e., who he is) remains crucial for his work (i.e., what he does). We put our faith in an unchanging Savior who is unchanging in his love toward us.

Application

In some sense, other creatures, such as angels, can be called immutable. Those angels who can no longer fall from grace remain in that state only because of God's power and grace, not because of their own nature. In contrast, God is holy, blessed, and good because of who he is by nature. Like angels, redeemed sinners are made and remain holy, blessed, and good because of God alone, namely through his graces given to them in Christ.

In heaven the redeemed will be immutable in some regard but not in the sense that they never change. As humans we shall always be changing—even our ability to learn more about God will grow. But we will be immutable in the sense that we can never, ever fall from grace. We shall be immutably blessed:

> And I heard a loud voice from the throne saying, "Behold, the dwelling place of God is with man. He will dwell with them, and they will be his people, and God himself will be with them as their God. He will wipe away every tear from their eyes, and death shall be no more, neither shall there be mourning, nor crying, nor pain anymore, for the former things have passed away." (Rev. 21:3–4)

For those who belong to Christ by faith, that immutable love and its effects begin now in this life (Rom. 8:1). We are the recipients of God's love before we love him (1 John 4:10). Our love for him may wax and wane in imperfection, but God's love for us remains as unchanging as his very being. Isaiah speaks of God's "everlasting love" (Isa. 54:8), declaring that even if the mountains are removed, God's "steadfast love" will never depart from his people (v. 10). The love of God comes to us in Christ Jesus (Eph. 1:3–14). His Son does not add to or cause the Father's love but does bring it out to us. As a result, the Father's love must be unchanging toward us; otherwise, he would have to stop loving his Son.

Bavinck wonderfully captures the relationship between God's unchangeability and the guarantee of our salvation:

God does not simply call himself "the One who is" and offer no explanation of his aseity, but states expressly what and how he is. Then how and what will he be? That is not something one can say in a word or describe in an additional phrase, but "he will be what he will be." That sums up everything. This addition is still general and indefinite, but for that reason also rich and full of deep meaning. . . . [H]e will be everything to and for his people. It is not a new and strange God who comes to them by Moses, but the God of the fathers, the Unchangeable One, the Faithful One, the eternally Self-consistent One, who never leaves or forsakes his people. . . . He is unchangeable in his grace, in his love, in his assistance, who will be what he is because he is always himself.[5]

[Meditate on this truth: God will be what he is because he is always himself—unchanging in his love toward us because he cannot be anything else to those who are in Christ.]

7

GOD IS INDEPENDENT

How precious is your steadfast love, O God!
>   The children of mankind take refuge in the
>   shadow of your wings.
They feast on the abundance of your house,
>   and you give them drink from the river of your
>   delights.
For with you is the fountain of life;
>   in your light do we see light.

Psalm 36:7–9

Doctrine

God's independence refers to his self-existence and self-sufficiency. This divine attribute means that God is ontologically independent from the created order and all created beings. He is not in need of us, but we are in need of him. We should not imagine that God is therefore unable to relate to his created beings. But we must be clear that we depend on him—and can depend on him—because he does not depend on anyone or anything.

Aseity is the idea that God derives his existence entirely from himself. It expresses God's self-sufficiency in terms of his being, which implies his utter and complete independence in all things.

God is derived from nothing. As the purest act (i.e., a completely actualized being), he has existence by and from himself alone. God is not his own cause, for he has no cause. He simply is. All his perfections are characterized by independence insofar as no single attribute can possibly be augmented or diminished. Because of God's independence, all creatures are derived from him as the source of all life. All life outside God depends on him.

Herman Bavinck offers one of the richest descriptions of God's aseity:

> God is exclusively from himself, not in the sense of being self-caused but being from eternity to eternity who he is, being not becoming. God is absolute being, the fullness of being, and therefore also eternally and absolutely independent in his existence, in his perfections, in all his works, the first and the last, the sole cause and final goal of all things. In this aseity of God, conceived not only as having being from himself but also as the fullness of being, all the other perfections are included.[1]

Anselm offers a similar take:

> But, in no wise does the supreme Nature exist through another, nor is it later or less than itself or anything else. Therefore, the supreme Nature could be created neither by itself, nor by another; nor could itself or any other be the matter whence it should be created; nor did it assist itself in any way; nor did anything assist it to be what it was not before.[2]

God's independence is his sufficiency. From his self-sufficiency are enough gifts, both natural and supernatural, to satisfy all creatures that shall ever come into existence. The Father, Son, and Holy Spirit all satisfy each other. Because they eternally and unchangeably do so in loving communion, they can satisfy others with whom they commune in love. If there were infinite worlds of loving creatures, all desiring happiness in God, he could as easily bless all as he could one.

As a living being, God is "the fountain of life" (Ps. 36:9):

See now that I, even I, am he,
    and there is no god beside me;
I kill and I make alive;
    I wound and I heal;
    and there is none that can deliver out of my hand.
For I lift up my hand to heaven
    and swear, As I live forever,
if I sharpen my flashing sword
    and my hand takes hold on judgment,
I will take vengeance on my adversaries
    and will repay those who hate me. (Deut. 32:39–41)

[He is all life, so that all outside him derive life from him. God does not need the world. He creates, gives, and sustains freely. As all life comes from him, he also possesses power over death; he kills and makes alive. In perpetual action, living and moving, he is simply that: the living God] (Isa. 37:17). "In him we live and move and have our being" (Acts 17:28; cf. v. 25). Having life and full knowledge in himself, he possesses the ultimate blessed life. True life is the blessed life.

In several ways, God's life differs from our life. For example, his life is his own, but our life we borrow from him. His life is infinite, being eternal, without beginning or end, but our life is finite, having a beginning and an end (in this world). God's life is perfect and blessed, but ours is imperfect. Because of his self-existence, immutability, and eternity, God lives at once, but we live over time, progressing. His life is all that he is: blessed, wise, all-knowing, all-powerful, and so forth. As a result, God lives necessarily, but we do not. We serve an immortal God (Rom. 1:23; 1 Tim. 1:17; 6:16). We come into this world because of his free decision to create.

Divine life necessitates God's all-sufficiency. This vital truth assures us that having an eternally, unchangeably, infinitely, blessedly all-sufficient God frees us from any worry as to whether he can satisfy our needs. Indeed he can, because he remains perfectly satisfied in himself. Such a principle helps us to understand the Father's relationship to the Son.

Christ's Dependence

The Son of God, according to his divine nature, possesses divine life in himself. The Father, Son, and Holy Spirit are all self-existent; they all share in the same undivided essence. Thus, there is one God in three persons.

We find the glory of the gospel not only in Christ's revelation of the Father and his purposes but also in the Son freely and willingly giving up his rights as God in order to become a servant (Phil. 2:5–11). As a servant, the Son became totally dependent on the Father for his spiritual life: "For as the Father has life in himself, so he has granted the Son also to have life in himself" (John 5:26). This verse may reflect something also about his eternal generation whereby the Father eternally and ineffably communicates life to the Son. But John 5:26 should also, perhaps even exclusively, be taken as a statement of how the Father gives life to the God-man, Jesus Christ.

Elsewhere, Christ says, "As the living Father sent me, and I live because of the Father, so whoever feeds on me, he also will live because of me" (John 6:57). The Father communicates spiritual life not directly to us but through his Son, the "Author of life" (Acts 3:15). In Christ is life, and his life is the light of men (John 1:4).

The independence of God means he is able to give life even to the God-man. In his incarnate state, Christ only spoke the words the Father gave to him (John 12:49). Christ even claimed that he could "do nothing of his own accord, but only what he sees the Father doing" (John 5:19).

Christ, who, according to his divine nature, is eternally and unchangeably independent (1 John 5:20), became dependent on the Father in order that his children might share in that dependence. As such, Christ becomes our life (Col. 3:4). The independence of God necessitated the dependence of the God-man in his earthly state and forever demands the dependence of all those who are united to Christ.

Application

In view of God's independence and self-sufficiency, perhaps we wonder, why would he care about or bother with us if he remains entirely without need? God created us not because he needed us but because he loved us. He loved simply because he chose to do so. He loves us so fully that his desire for us is not so much that we live the "purpose-driven life" but that we live a wholly dependent life.

If Christ had to constantly depend on the Father when he walked this earth, insofar as he had the Spirit given to him from the Father without measure, then are we somehow exempt from this type of life? Dependence on the Independent One is likely a great deal more difficult than we imagine. In Christ's teaching in the Sermon on the Mount, he implores his disciples to ask, seek, and knock in order to receive (Matt. 7:7–8). God should not have to command us to ask him; we should be going to him daily, begging to be filled with his Spirit. We must become like little children, who depend entirely on him (Matt. 18:2–4).

God's all-sufficiency, because of his self-existence, therefore encourages believers. He who possesses all things in himself supplies our every need, ultimately through Christ: "And my God will supply every need of yours according to his riches in glory in Christ Jesus" (Phil. 4:19).

James actually chastises believers for their self-sufficiency. He rebukes them for wanting from the world what they can only obtain from God: "You desire and do not have, so you murder. You covet and cannot obtain, so you fight and quarrel. You do not have, because you do not ask. You ask and do not receive, because you ask wrongly, to spend it on your passions" (James 4:2–3). Instead, we who naturally lack wisdom should ask God, "who gives generously to all without reproach" (James 1:5). We believe, but we need to ask him to help our unbelief (Mark 9:24).

One of our fundamental problems as Christians is forgetting God's independence and all that it means for us in Christ. We rarely, if at all, meditate on his self-sufficiency, by which he can give us all we need through his beloved Son. How much more ought we to focus on the glorious truth that God wants to give us more than we even desire.

8

GOD IS OMNIPRESENT

Can a man hide himself in secret places so that I cannot see him? declares the LORD. Do I not fill heaven and earth? declares the LORD.

Jeremiah 23:24

Doctrine

We know God's omnipresence as the concept that he is everywhere. As a spirit, his omnipresence implies the immensity of his essence: "But will God indeed dwell on the earth? Behold, heaven and the highest heaven cannot contain you; how much less this house that I have built!" (1 Kings 8:27). Like Solomon, David also beautifully affirms the omnipresence of God:

Where shall I go from your Spirit?
    Or where shall I flee from your presence?
If I ascend to heaven, you are there!
    If I make my bed in Sheol, you are there!
If I take the wings of the morning
    and dwell in the uttermost parts of the sea,
even there your hand shall lead me,
    and your right hand shall hold me. (Ps. 139:7–10)

Historically, theologians have distinguished between God's

immensity and his omnipresence. Immensity refers to spatiality; omnipresence refers to his relation toward filled, or concrete, space. Immensity denies to God any spatial limitations; omnipresence explains God's disposition toward space. Or to put it another way, the immensity of God refers to his distinction from creation, while his omnipresence has in view his relation to the world, namely, that he "dwells" in all places in his created order.

God is infinite, but we are finite. Finite creatures exist in space; we are somewhere in space but not at the same time somewhere else. Unlike us, God is not bound in any way, whether by time or by space. If he were, he would not be God. As Edward Leigh observes, God is "neither shut up in any place, nor shut out from any place."[1] In the whole, vast created universe, of which we still know so very little, God is perfectly and powerfully present in every place; he fills all space as God. There is nowhere where God is not present.

In relating God's omnipresence to his other attributes, Stephen Charnock maintains, "As eternity is the perfection whereby he hath neither beginning nor end, immutability is the perfection whereby he hath neither increase nor diminution, so immensity or omnipresence is that whereby he hath neither bounds nor limitation."[2]

Also, in affirming God's omnipresence, Charnock speaks of three ways that something may be present or in a place:

1. Circumscriptively (of physical bodies as circumscribed): For example, the hand, belonging to the body, is not in the same particular place as the foot.

2. Definitely (of angels and spirits as finite beings): We speak of definite presence when we say that angels are in one point and not another at the same time.

3. Repletively (of God as filling all places): God is repletively present because he is not limited by space. As God is infinite, he fills all things: "He is from the height of

the heavens to the bottom of the deeps, in every point of the world, and in the whole circle of it, yet not limited by it, but beyond it."[3]

The omnipresence of God refers not only to his presence everywhere but also to his infinite and powerful influence over all things in all places. All things in heaven and on earth are subject to him by his power, since he providentially sustains all things. Likewise, such subjection manifests itself in the fact that God knows all things, implying his presence in all places. As Charnock says, "His power reaches all, and his knowledge pierces all."[4]

In the Bible, the doctrine of God's creation does not mean simply that God made the earth out of nothing but also that he preserves the earth according to his wisdom and power and goodness. To preserve all things according to all his perfections, he must be present everywhere. In sustaining all creatures, he cares for each as if he or she were the only one. Just as all times are a moment in relation to his eternity, all people and places are a point in relation to his being because of his omnipresence.

While God is present everywhere, he manifests his presence in different ways. In heaven, God's presence toward the saints delights and comforts them. In hell, God's presence toward the damned terrifies and torments them. God is as present in heaven as he is in hell, but he exhibits his presence differently in each place. Even on earth, we may speak of God being present in a special manner, as Jacob did: "Then Jacob awoke from his sleep and said, 'Surely the LORD is in this place, and I did not know it.' And he was afraid and said, 'How awesome is this place! This is none other than the house of God, and this is the gate of heaven'" (Gen. 28:16–17). Similarly, whether in the tabernacle or the temple, his covenantal presence was peculiarly revealed to his people in a way not shown to others (Ex. 25:8–9; 1 Kings 8).

Christ with Us

Divine omnipresence finds its focal point in the person of Christ, our Immanuel, "God with us" (Matt. 1:23). Herman Bavinck, quoting Augustine, makes the important point that

> God dwells in all his creatures, but not in all alike. All things are indeed "in him" . . . but not necessarily "with him." . . . God does not dwell on earth as he does in heaven, in animals as in humans, . . . in the wicked as in the devout, in the church as he does in Christ. . . . In Christ he dwells uniquely: by personal union.[5]

In the person of Christ, the omnipresence of God toward his people comes to its intended goal. As the God-man, Christ is in one sense limited because of his finite human nature but in another sense not limited by his human nature because of his divine nature. The latter transcends the former in Christ as a person. That is, the eternal Son of God became flesh; his divine nature was united to but not contained within the human nature. Christians must understand and embrace this principle.

After his resurrection, Christ promised his followers that he would be with them "always" (Matt. 28:20). This takes place through the abiding presence of the Holy Spirit, the Helper and Comforter, who carries on the ministry of the ascended Christ in the lives of believers. Everything about the Spirit's work in the church is based on Christ's resurrection, ascension, and enthronement as the exalted Son of God. The presence of the Spirit in the believer is the presence of Christ (Rom. 8:9–10). Paul brings out this concept beautifully in Ephesians 3:16–17, where he informs Christians that as they are "strengthened with power through his Spirit in [their] inner being," it is so that "Christ may dwell in [their] hearts through faith." The roles of the Spirit and Christ are used interchangeably not in the sense that the two persons are fused into one or that one person becomes the other but in the sense that Paul is affirming the presence of Jesus through the work of the Spirit.

This teaching helps us to make sense of John 14:16–18:

> And I will ask the Father, and he will give you another Helper, to be with you forever, even the Spirit of truth, whom the world cannot receive, because it neither sees him nor knows him. You know him, for he dwells with you and will be in you. I will not leave you as orphans; I will come to you.

Christ's departure is gain for his disciples (John 16:7) because by sending the Spirit, Christ returns to his people in a more intimate way than was possible in his bodily presence. Thus, turning again to Matthew 28:20, we can say that Christ is speaking not simply about divine omnipresence but more specifically about his covenantal presence among his people as the promise of the new covenant is fulfilled.

Application

Most Christians affirm God's attribute of omnipresence, but their actions sometimes betray this belief. Sin does that. When Adam first sinned, he thought he could hide from God (Gen. 3:10). We too try to hide from his presence, but this is a futile flight, says the writer of Hebrews: "And no creature is hidden from his sight, but all are naked and exposed to the eyes of him to whom we must give account" (Heb. 4:13). Other times we simply forget in everyday life, in the good times and bad, that Christ is with us, for he "will never leave [us] nor forsake [us]" (Heb. 13:5).

As Christians, we sometimes fall into the realm of practical atheism, affirming God with our minds and denying him with our hearts. What is worse, Christians commit certain sins in the presence of God that they would never dream of doing in the presence of others. In this age of Internet pornography, which enslaves so many in the church, the vast majority commit this sin in private, not in public. Imagine that: God's presence has less influence on us than that of mere humans.

Far from being mere high-end theology for those in ivory

towers, the study of God's attributes should bring us to the place where we are humbled to the very core of our being. But the omnipresence of God need not terrify us as believers, even if the ungodly flee his presence. Our fear as Christians should be one not of dread or terror but of reverential awe.

As John Murray notes so well, "The fear of God which is the basis of godliness, and in which godliness may be said to consist, is much more inclusive and determinative than the fear of God's judgment."[6] A Christian fear of God keeps his awesome nature before our eyes continually, reminding us of his presence everywhere. He sees us, takes note of us, and most importantly, dwells in us (1 John 4:16) for our sanctification (Heb. 13:5; see also James 4:8).

When Christians focus on God's omnipresence, they are convinced of not only a general but also a special and covenantal presence, particularly in the person of Christ (Eph. 3:16–17). As we are tempted, we must remember that he is present with us to help us. We must also remember that because Christ is present, if we fall into temptation, we are, in a sense, implicating him in our sin. As we meditate on the great price Christ paid on the cross so that he could one day dwell in our hearts, that should motivate us to flee sin.

So in the end, we hold not only to the indisputable fact that God is everywhere present but also to the teaching that he is intimately among his people in Christ as our all-sufficiency, hope, joy, and comfort. In this way we can live our lives in the power of the One who was raised in power (Rom. 1:4).

9

GOD IS OMNISCIENT

Great is our Lord, and abundant in power;
his understanding is beyond measure.

Psalm 147:5

Doctrine

The doctrine of God's knowledge has occasioned much debate in the church over the centuries. Some have reasoned that if he knows all that can be known, how can the actions of his creatures, especially humans, be free? In an effort to protect free will, some theologians have thus argued that God cannot possibly know all that can be known. But if he does not know all things, then he is like man: ignorant (i.e., lacking knowledge). Not surprisingly, based on a careful study of the Scriptures, Reformed theologians have always insisted that God is omniscient, or "all-knowing." Indeed, it is to our great advantage, not detriment, that the infinite and eternal God knows all that can be known.

If God is infinite, then so are all his attributes, including his knowledge. There is no limit to what he knows, and there is nothing he needs to learn. He knows all things in and of himself with a perfect knowledge of all things past, present, and future (Job 28:24; 37:16; Ps. 94:9–10). Regarding his knowledge of things future, we speak of *prescience* or *foreknowledge*, even if his

77

eternality makes the use of these terms technically improper. Still, we can say he has foreknowledge insofar as he knows the future, because he has ordained it.

But he does not merely know all things past, present, and future; his knowledge involves his infinite wisdom or understanding of all things. In knowing, God is doing; in doing, God's wisdom is manifested. So the all-knowing God always does what is best as the all-wise (*omnisapient*) God. We should constantly keep in mind that one attribute cannot be divorced from another; the one informs the other. Thus, his knowledge is his wisdom is his power is his goodness, and so forth.

In knowing himself perfectly, God cannot help but love and delight in himself. Thus, he loves his infinite knowledge in the same way he loves his infinite power. His perfect understanding makes him infinitely blessed. God's self-love must be present in terms of the three persons of the Trinity both loving the divine nature and experiencing mutual love among themselves.

In the words of Stephen Charnock,

> God knows all other things, whether they be possible, past, present, or future; whether they be things that he can do, but will never do, or whether they be things that he hath done, but are not now; things that are now in being, or things that are not now existing, that lie in the womb of their proper and immediate causes. If his understanding be infinite, he then knows all things whatsoever that can be known, else his understanding would have bounds, and what hath limits is not infinite, but finite.[1]

God's complete knowledge of all (theoretically) possible worlds necessitates his perfect knowledge of this world, which he created by the word of his power. He also has perfect knowledge of the present, even though, strictly speaking, there exists only the present in God, because he sees all things in his eternal "instant" (i.e., at once). Technically, we ought not to speak of God knowing the past and the future, because such do not exist for him. As Bavinck attests, "[God] knows all things in and of and by himself. For that reason his knowledge is undivided, simple, unchangeable, eternal. He knows all things instantaneously, simultaneously, from eternity; all things are eternally present to his mind's eye."[2] He knows all things as decreed by him.

Why were God's prophets, such as Isaiah (see Isa. 41:4), able to infallibly predict future events? Because God, who knows the future perfectly, revealed to his prophets what would surely take place. In contrasting his glory with the idols of Canaanite and Mesopotamian religions, Yahweh declares,

> Let them bring them, and tell us
> what is to happen.
> Tell us the former things, what they are,
> that we may consider them,
> that we may know their outcome;
> or declare to us the things to come. (Isa. 41:22)

Or later God says,

> Who is like me? Let him proclaim it.
> Let him declare and set it before me,
> since I appointed an ancient people.
> Let them declare what is to come, and what will happen.
> (Isa. 44:7)

God can declare the future because he knows and has ordained it. If we watch a mystery film and tape it, knowing the outcome, we can sit down with friends who have not yet seen the film and can predict the ending based on knowledge we possess but they do not. Similarly, God's knowledge enables him to accurately predict the end result, because he infinitely knows what will happen as the One who has declared the end from the beginning:

> Remember this and stand firm,
> recall it to mind, you transgressors,
> remember the former things of old;

79

for I am God, and there is no other;
    I am God, and there is none like me,
declaring the end from the beginning
    and from ancient times things not yet done,
saying, "My counsel shall stand,
    and I will accomplish all my purpose,"
calling a bird of prey from the east,
    the man of my counsel from a far country.
I have spoken, and I will bring it to pass;
    I have purposed, and I will do it. (Isa. 46:8–11)

Those rejecting this view of God's knowledge endeavor to protect human freedom. For example, the Roman Catholic Jesuit theologian Luis de Molina (1535–1600) proposed the idea of *middle knowledge*, later embraced by the well-known but not always well-understood Protestant Jacob Arminius (1560–1609). This view became known as *Molinism*.

In short, Molina believed that God could know, prior to choosing individuals, what a given number of human beings, who are free, will do in certain circumstances. In other words, he knows both what actually will happen and what might possibly happen under given conditions. As a result, God elects based on his "middle knowledge" that certain individuals will respond favorably to the gospel under specific circumstances. In the end, God does not elect independently and unconditionally in Christ but "reacts" to the foreknown choice of a finite being.

If God's foreknowledge depends on future conditionals, it needs to be asked whether he remains ignorant in some sense. God "sees" what would happen based on a conditional future and then chooses based on what he "sees" take place in a purely conditional world. In this scheme, God knows conditionals conditionally. In sum, Molinism introduces a separate category, in which the human decision becomes the causal factor that determines the event.

Open theism, as advocated by Clark Pinnock and Greg Boyd,

attempts to address the problems of Molinism by proposing that God has left the future partly open in that some of the possible choices that humans may make are left in just that state, possible and uncertain. In other words, God does not know the future exhaustively. So, says Boyd, God

> created a world in which the future is partially open, comprised of possibilities rather than settled facts. And God did this, in our view, precisely because he didn't want to unilaterally determine all that comes to pass. (How boring that would be for God!) God rather wanted to populate this cosmos with free agents, thereby creating the possibility of genuine love, adventure, and yes, the risk of sin and evil.[3]

Open theists affirm God's omniscience while denying his foreknowledge, which actually obliterates the concept of omniscience, since God's knowledge is not certain and since, beyond this, he can change his mind, can learn, and is even said to take risks (because he does not know the future exhaustively). "In a cosmos populated by free agents," claims Boyd, "the outcome of things—even divine decisions—is often uncertain."[4] In summary, for Boyd (contrary to what he might claim), God is not God.

Christ's Knowledge

We should not be so quick to assume that Christ's supernatural knowledge in the New Testament proved his divinity by proving his omniscience. In one well-known passage, Christ makes the claim that "all things have been handed over to me by my Father, and no one knows the Son except the Father, and no one knows the Father except the Son and anyone to whom the Son chooses to reveal him" (Matt. 11:27). This verse does not suggest that Christ knows the Father because of his divinity, even though that is certainly true, as taught elsewhere (John 1:1–2). Instead, this verse teaches that the knowledge that the Father gave the Son can be accessed at least in part by believers: "and anyone to whom the Son choose to reveal him."

Most references to Christ's knowledge in the New Testament are references to the abundant knowledge that the Father imparted to him according to his human nature (see John 21:17). The Father bestowed on Christ knowledge and wisdom for Christ to execute his office as Mediator: "in whom are hidden all the treasures of wisdom and knowledge" (Col. 2:3).

Why is this distinction important? Apart from the knowledge communicated to Christ, we could have no knowledge of God. Christ makes knowledge of God possible because he knew God and revealed the Father to us (Luke 10:21–22).

So God's infinite knowledge remains the basis for him imparting to Christ all kinds of knowledge, such as the following:

1. The inner workings of people's hearts: "[Jesus] said to him the third time, 'Simon, son of John, do you love me?' Peter was grieved because he said to him the third time, 'Do you love me?' and he said to him, 'Lord, you know everything; you know that I love you.' Jesus said to him, 'Feed my sheep'" (John 21:17).

2. Hidden facts of people's lives: "The woman answered him, 'I have no husband.' Jesus said to her, 'You are right in saying, "I have no husband"; for you have had five husbands, and the one you now have is not your husband. What you have said is true'" (John 4:17–18).

3. Future events: "Then Jesus, knowing all that would happen to him, came forward and said to them, 'Whom do you seek?'" (John 18:4); "Jesus said to him, 'Truly, I tell you, this very night, before the rooster crows, you will deny me three times'" (Matt. 26:34).

Christ had access to this type of knowledge because of God's omniscience. He could have depended on his own divine resources, so to speak, but his humiliation in the incarnation necessitated a willingness to completely and constantly depend on the Father to teach him all that he needed to know. Very often, the Father's teaching enabled Christ to supernaturally know things that proved his messianic identity.

In his exaltation, Christ received from the Father through the Spirit the greatest capacity of knowledge ever received by a human being. According to his human nature and as part of his reward from the Father, the Spirit revealed to Christ all that could be known about God's kingdom, purposes, and people. The knowledge that Christ possesses in his glorified humanity is utterly beyond our comprehension.

We can only marvel at the idea of a human being knowing the thoughts of all humanity. As our sympathetic High Priest, he must not only hear our prayers but also know our weaknesses, temptations, and desires. This knowledge enables him to sympathize (Heb. 4:15). But gloriously, he knows all these things not only according to his divine nature but also according to his human nature. We too in glory will have our natures transformed so that our ability to know the things of God, Christ, nature, and all reality will be so far advanced from our present state. We will indeed "share" in the knowledge of God by the Spirit through Christ, the Revealer of all truth, yet without ever approaching his omniscience.

Application

God and Christ know the thoughts and intentions of men, as well a thousand years ago as now. This remains the peculiar right and privilege of God alone. His omniscience has many practical applications to the Christian life, but I want to highlight one in particular.

As Christians we can, sometimes unwittingly but nonetheless sinfully, act as if we were God by making judgments about others without the requisite knowledge that enables us to make a sound judgment. While Christ warns against a hypercritical or judgmental spirit coupled with a failure to deal with one's own sin

(Matt. 7:1), Christians must sometimes judge (see Matt. 7:15–20; 18:15–20; 24:23–26). But judging others can be dangerous, in part because we often lack the information to do so. Christ judged appropriately because he had perfect knowledge—given to him from above—for correct judgments (John 8:44).

The judgments God and Christ make are based on the knowledge we so frequently lack. We should not make a judgment unless we have the correct facts. We also must avoid judging unfairly. God judges not simply because he knows all things but because he lovingly knows all things and never makes unfair judgments. He is never biased, as we are. If we make judgments, we must not only have the facts but must also be motivated by love. And of course, should we judge, we should also be firmly persuaded that it is necessary for us to intervene and make a judgment. God judges based on his knowledge but also based on his sovereign dominion (i.e., his right to judge).

Remember, the Pharisees judged Christ: "And when the Pharisees saw this, they said to his disciples, 'Why does your teacher eat with tax collectors and sinners?'" (Matt. 9:11). Elsewhere, we read Christ saying, "The Son of Man came eating and drinking, and they say, 'Look at him! A glutton and a drunkard, a friend of tax collectors and sinners!' Yet wisdom is justified by her deeds" (Matt. 11:19). Such judgments manifested ignorance of Christ's gracious redemption, exposed a self-righteous blindness to sin, and were devoid of love. All these we must avoid but so often do not.

When we are tempted to make a judgment without sufficient facts, we are better off leaving such judgments to God. We can entrust all things to him who judges justly (1 Pet. 2:23). Lacking the proper knowledge we need and being mindful of God's grace to us in Christ, we can respond in love toward others by erring on the side of caution. Sometimes we do best to remain silent. We know that in the end, God will, because of his vast omniscience, right every wrong. He is able, willing, and determined to do so.

10

GOD IS OMNIPOTENT

It is he who made the earth by his power,
    who established the world by his wisdom,
    and by his understanding stretched out the
        heavens.
When he utters his voice, there is a tumult of
        waters in the heavens,
    and he makes the mist rise from the ends of the
        earth.
He makes lightning for the rain,
    and he brings forth the wind from his
        storehouses.
                  Jeremiah 10:12–13

Doctrine

Affirming God's almighty power or *omnipotence* remains as important as attesting that he exists. A God without such power is not worth worshiping. We might as well be atheists. God exercises justice and mercy precisely because of his unbounded capability to do so.

God possesses unlimited power as the infinitely Powerful One, which explains why the Bible uses "power" as a proper name for God: "And Jesus said, 'I am, and you will see the Son of Man seated at the right hand of Power, and coming with the clouds of heaven'" (Mark 14:62). Because he is infinitely powerful, no such thing as "hard work" exists for God. Creating the world remains as easy as creating a pebble because of his infinite power.

The Scriptures often contrast God's power with human power and our conceptions of what is possible:

> Is anything too hard for the LORD? At the appointed time I will return to you, about this time next year, and Sarah shall have a son. (Gen. 18:14)

> For nothing will be impossible with God. (Luke 1:37)

> With man this is impossible, but with God all things are possible. (Matt. 19:26)

God's power refers to that force or ability by which he acts. He can do whatever he pleases. He is "mighty in strength" (Job 9:4) and "great in power" (Job 37:23). More specifically, his power may be understood in two ways, either as authority or as strength. One may theoretically have one without the other, but God possesses both. As Charnock attests,

> The power of God is that ability and strength whereby He can bring to pass whatsoever He pleases, whatsoever His infinite wisdom may direct, and whatsoever the infinite purity of His will may resolve. . . . God's power is like Himself: infinite, eternal, incomprehensible; it can neither be checked, restrained, nor frustrated by the creature.[1]

Thus, God's power remains identical with his being (Mark 14:62).

When discussing God's power, theologians typically distinguish between his absolute and ordained power.[2] *Absolute power* refers to what God may possibly do but does not necessarily do. He could create a billion worlds of living creatures without deciding to actually do it. God's *ordained power* denotes what he actually decreed according to his will and then providentially accomplishes. With such language we are not setting forth two distinct powers in God but rather understanding his omnipotence by way of application (ordained power) and nonapplication (absolute power).

God's power must also be understood as exercised according to or "governed" by his nature. His power must be a good power. When he speaks—an act of his power—he speaks truthfully. God cannot lie (Titus 1:2). So, hypothetically speaking, if he made a spaceship that he later dissolved, it would be eternally true that God had made a spaceship. He could not say that he did not make a spaceship if he had in fact made a spaceship. Nothing true, according to his designation of truth, can ever be described as false. He could not call the Devil, who is pure evil, good. God cannot act in a way that compromises his holiness or justice or goodness or truth.

On occasion, the Bible explicitly draws attention to God's absolute and ordained power, sometimes mentioning both in the same passage. As an example of his absolute power, John the Baptist declares to the unrepentant Pharisees and Sadducees: "And do not presume to say to yourselves, 'We have Abraham as our father' for I tell you, God is able from these stones to raise up children for Abraham" (Matt. 3:9). As far as we know, God did not in fact raise up from the stones "children for Abraham," but he could have according to his absolute power.

God's Power in Relation to Christ

In Matthew 26:53–54, Christ describes both God's absolute and ordained power: "Do you think that I cannot appeal to my Father, and he will at once send me more than twelve legions of angels? But how then should the Scriptures be fulfilled, that it must be so?" God could have rescued Christ from his passion, according to his absolute power, but he did not do so, according to his ordained power. We find a hint of this doctrine in Christ's temptation. Satan tempted Jesus to turn stones into bread to prove that he was the

Son of God. But Christ, who could have done so, did not do so, because Scripture, not the Devil, was his rule of life. What Jesus himself could theoretically have done (Matt. 4:3–4) was not the point. The point was what Jesus was supposed to do under the rule of God.

God shows his power by sending his Son to be crucified in weakness (2 Cor. 13:4). Paul says of the one who freely embraced weakness that he "was declared to be the Son of God in power according to the Spirit of holiness by his resurrection from the dead, Jesus Christ our Lord" (Rom. 1:4). So the gospel, which has in view the weakness and power of Christ (necessarily joined together) according to his two states (humiliation and exaltation), is "the power of God for salvation" (Rom. 1:16). Paul became a minister of the gospel by the "working of [God's] power" (Eph. 3:7). And this good news comes to God's people so that they may be "strengthened with power through his Spirit" (Eph. 3:16).

Application

We must resist the temptation to live in the theoretical world of God's absolute power. Instead, we should trust in his ordained power. The promises and prescriptions of Scripture relate to God's ordained power, though they do not always end up being synonymous. The distinction between God's absolute and ordained power has implications for the Christian life.

According to God's absolute power, he could sanctify every Christian congregation immediately by the power of his Spirit, quite apart from preaching, the reading of God's Word, and the sacraments. But according to his ordained power, he has not chosen to do so. Rather, he has ordained means to accomplish ends. So we must put away such unbiblical exclamations as "Why doesn't God just take us all to heaven now and destroy the world?" Instead, we can rest content in God's sovereign plan for us and the world.

If ministers keep a "close watch" on themselves and on "the teaching," and if they persist in doing so, then they can expect to save themselves and their hearers (1 Tim. 4:16; see also Rom. 10:14–15). This is a promise with prescriptions. The fulfillment of this promise comes from God's power but not apart from the ordained means (e.g., preaching the truth) that he dictated for the salvation of the elect.

Equally, God ordained that prayer should accomplish certain ends. If we do not pray, we will not receive (Matt. 7:7–11; James 4:2). True, God could accomplish all without the prayers of his people, but he has not ordained such a remedy. He works powerfully through the prayers of his weak people (Rom. 8:26–27).

This distinction informs the way we carry out our various callings. For example, if we fail to raise our children in the fear and admonition of the Lord (Eph. 6:4), we have no reason to hope in God's covenantal promises for them. I am not suggesting that we can be perfect parents, never making a mistake. But there is a difference between a faithful parent obeying and trusting God and a carnal parent presuming on God's gracious work. We must raise our children according to the demands of the covenant, not the secret will of God (Deut. 29:29).

Moreover, a Christian wife might content herself with the possibility that God could convert her husband as he walks down the street listening to opera music. Instead, she ought to look to 1 Peter 3:1–2 as her hope: "Likewise, wives, be subject to your own husbands, so that even if some do not obey the word, they may be won without a word by the conduct of their wives, when they see your respectful and pure conduct."

Amazingly, God's ordained power makes use of human means. And these means are rather ordinary, such as preaching, prayer, admonition, and godliness. This power comes to us through our powerful Savior, crucified in weakness and now exalted as our prophet and priest to equip us with his power for every good work (2 Tim. 3:17; Heb. 13:21).

11

GOD IS YAHWEH

God spoke to Moses and said to him, "I am the
LORD. I appeared to Abraham, to Isaac, and to
Jacob, as God Almighty, but by my name the LORD
I did not make myself known to them."

Exodus 6:2–3

Doctrine

We can learn about God by understanding the meaning of his
name as revealed in Scripture. His name is identical with his attributes in terms of how he manifests them to us in his Word. God
does not need a proper name. His self-appointed name describes
him not as he exists within himself but as he reveals himself and
relates to his creatures. Thus, by using names, God accommodates
himself to his creatures and reveals himself to us.

God's names function as a synonym for his character, the sum
of his attributes (Ex. 20:7; Ps. 8:1). Correspondingly, to know his
name is to know him (Ex. 6:3). While they are anthropomorphic,
these names do not originate with humanity, as if we were in any
position to name God. Rather, these names disclose to us God's
personal existence, his attributes, and his glorious being. Although
nameless within himself, God in his revelation has many names.
We have chosen to focus on just one in this chapter, the "LORD,"

or Yahweh (sometimes also referred to as Jehovah or YHWH), which is used roughly five thousand times in the Old Testament.

The etymology of Yahweh has been discussed a great deal through the course of church history, with no firm consensus on all the details. Coming from the root *hwy* or *hyh* (meaning "to be, be at hand, exist, come to pass"), the name of God may be understood in light of God's works rather than the name's sheer etymology. To ask for God's name is to ask for his character:

> Then Moses said to God, "If I come to the people of Israel and say to them, 'The God of your fathers has sent me to you,' and they ask me, 'What is his name?' what shall I say to them?" God said to Moses, "I AM WHO I AM." And he said, "Say this to the people of Israel, 'I AM has sent me to you.'" (Ex. 3:13–14)

With the revelation of his "name," we must remember that no one name can fully reveal who God is. Nevertheless, this revelation tells us a great deal about God. *Yahweh* reveals his nature, particularly that he is not only self-existent ("I am") but also unchangeable ("I will be what I will be"). God's immutability (i.e., unchangeability) carried no small consequence for the Israelites, who depended on his covenant faithfulness. This proclamation was the high point of God's revelation up to that time in redemptive history.

In the context of Exodus, the name Yahweh points to his covenant faithfulness: "I will take you to be my people, and I will be your God, and you shall know that I am the LORD your God, who has brought you out from under the burdens of the Egyptians" (Ex. 6:7; see also 3:7–9, 13–14; 6:1). His name also reveals his sovereignty and glory: "that they may know that you alone, whose name is the LORD, are the Most High over all the earth" (Ps. 83:18). As the Lord, Yahweh is the everlasting, omniscient, omnipotent God:

> Have you not known? Have you not heard?
> The LORD is the everlasting God,
>> the Creator of the ends of the earth.

> He does not faint or grow weary;
>> his understanding is unsearchable. (Isa. 40:28)

His name remains synonymous with his eternal being (Isa. 41:4; 44:6). As the Glorious One, Yahweh expresses jealousy for the worship of his people and the glory of his name: "I am the LORD; that is my name; my glory I give to no other, nor my praise to carved idols" (Isa. 42:8).

His name can strike terror in hearts. Yahweh speaks in thunder and shoots lightning across the sky (Ex. 19:16–19; 20:18). He reveals his presence by fire (Ex. 13:21) and controls the elements of the earth, such as the sea (Ex. 14:21). Yet as noted above, Yahweh deals with his people as the God of the covenant. He creates and preserves all things, but in a special way, he sustains his people according to his promises to them. Thus, the name Yahweh is peculiarly significant to God's people because it represents his covenant-keeping faithfulness toward them.

Christ Is Yahweh

After Christ fulfilled the work that the Father gave him to do, God bestowed on him the divine name:

> Therefore God has highly exalted him and bestowed on him the name that is above every name, so that at the name of Jesus every knee should bow, in heaven and on earth and under the earth, and every tongue confess that Jesus Christ is Lord, to the glory of God the Father. (Phil. 2:9–11)

The name is not explicitly given, but there is good reason to assume that it refers to Yahweh. Jesus has perfectly represented the Father on earth as "the image of the invisible God" (Col. 1:15). As such, he has the public authority to receive the highest blessing possible: the name above every name. What name could be higher than Yahweh and all that it means?

Not only Paul but also John uses language from Isaiah that

enforces this basic theological point about Christ's exalted status. In Isaiah we read the following claims by Yahweh:

> I, the LORD, the first,
>> and with the last; I am he. (Isa. 41:4)

> I am the first and I am the last;
>> besides me there is no god. (Isa. 44:6)

> I am he; I am the first,
>> and I am the last. (Isa. 48:12)

Now look at John's description of Jesus in Revelation:

> Fear not, I am the first and the last, and the living one. (Rev. 1:17–18)

> And to the angel of the church in Smyrna write: "The words of the first and the last, who died and came to life." (Rev. 2:8)

> I am the Alpha and the Omega, the first and the last, the beginning and the end. (Rev. 22:13)

As these passages in Revelation show, Jesus's name speaks to his prerogatives as the immutable, eternal, and living God. The exalted Christ bears the name of Yahweh.

Application

God names himself to bless his people. He names himself to instruct his people. God does not need to name himself, but he chooses freely to condescend in order to give us knowledge of God's being and his purposes toward us. Remarkably, while God does not need to name himself, he does name his Son. The God-man has the peculiar dignity of being recognized as Yahweh. In light of that truth, we can be as sure of Christ's heart toward us as we can be of God's heart toward the Israelites when he brought them out of Egypt.

As the exalted Messiah and High Priest interceding in the heavenly places, Jesus is trustworthy. Christ's purposes, and thus his teachings, remain the same toward believers. He is unchangeable in his purposes. Hence, the author of Hebrews assures his readers of this aspect of Christ's ministry: "Jesus Christ is the same yesterday and today and forever" (Heb. 13:8).

If God is able to bestow a name on Jesus, he is also able to bestow a name on those who remain faithful to the end like Jesus did. In Revelation 2:17, we are told that believers will receive a new name. This promise extends to all of God's faithful servants and is not limited to the immediate recipients of John's letter. To receive this new name is to receive Christ's kingly name (Rev. 19:12–16). We are named in baptism, as we enter into a new relationship with God. At the end, we shall also receive a new name that will confirm to us our exalted status. Without this new name, we will not enter into the new heavens and the new earth.

12

GOD IS BLESSED

You make known to me the path of life;
in your presence there is fullness of joy;
at your right hand are pleasures forevermore.
Psalm 16:11

Doctrine

Of all of God's infinitely glorious attributes, perhaps his blessedness should cause us the most envy. In him exists a perfect union of all good things. He has an eternally infinite fullness, delight, and joy in himself. As completely self-sufficient, he needs nothing. Hence, Paul speaks of the "blessed" God (1 Tim. 1:11; 6:15).

If God were infinitely good but unable to effect good because he lacked power, that would make him miserable. If God were merciful and holy but lacked wisdom to save sinners without injustice to his mercy and holiness, he would also be miserable. If God were not triune, his love for himself would also make him miserable. Indeed, if God were eternal but lacked infinite knowledge, he would be more miserable than those in hell. As a perfect being, who is fully actualized in his being and whose attributes all gloriously harmonize with one another, he enjoys a most happy life. Where there reside infinite holiness, wisdom, goodness, power, knowledge, and so forth, there must be infinite blessedness.

Speaking of God's happiness, Benedict Pictet proclaims,

The life of God is most happy, since he is more than once called "blessed" God by Paul (1 Tim. 1:11; 6:15); and the validity of the reference will be clear to anyone who properly considers the concept of true happiness. For who would not call God happy, who is in need of nothing, finds all comfort in himself, and possesses all things; is free from evil, and filled with all good.[1]

Similarly, Edward Leigh maintains, "God's happiness is that Attribute whereby God has all fullness of delight and contentment in himself, and needs nothing out of himself to make him happy."[2] If there is any happiness outside God in this universe, it is a happiness derived from God. Indeed, "the human nature of Christ himself in heaven is not so; it lives in God, and God in it, in a full dependence on God, and receiving blessed and glorious communications from him."[3]

In addition, we must never consider the blessedness of God apart from the triunity of God. According to John Owen, "The blessedness of God consists in the ineffable mutual inbeing of the three holy persons in the same nature, with the immanent reciprocal actings of the Father and the Son in the eternal love and complacency of the Spirit."[4] God's blessedness involves his eternal and infinite joy over his essence. The Father, Son, and Spirit share in a personal love with each other that is blessed love. To know that God is happy should make us most happy.

More specifically, theologians have spoken of God's blessedness in terms of not just his abounding in all good things but also his being free from all miseries: "God is light, and in him is no darkness at all" (1 John 1:5). As such, his happiness is guaranteed by his infinite and unchangeable holiness. Others have carried this point further to affirm that God perfectly knows his blessedness. He desires nothing more than what he has because it is impossible for him to be more or less blessed than he is.

The blessedness of God is the fountain from which we drink. Because his blessedness abounds in all good things, when he created the world, he created all things good—and thus, blessed. For example, Adam's goodness issued forth in his happiness, especially since he knew God's love in making him good (1 John 4:8). Sin destroyed such bliss to bring misery. But God sent his Son to deal with sin and misery for the restorative purposes of making us like himself in a state of blessedness, happiness, contentment, fulfillment, and joy!

Christ's Blessedness

Was Christ joyful all the days of his life? Was the "man of sorrows" (Isa. 53:3) a man of joy at the same time? There is no reason to conclude that he was not always joyful during his earthly life. And if anyone had an excuse for being miserable, Christ did. But biblical joy in humans can coexist with biblical sorrow. Think of a funeral where a loved one has gone to be with the Lord. There we simultaneously possess joy and sorrow.

We can affirm Christ's continual earthly joy for several reasons:

1. He was filled with the Holy Spirit without measure (John 3:34), and the fruit of the Spirit includes "joy."
2. He was good and was free from sin; he is the Righteous One, with every reason to love his personal holiness, which he received in abundance from his Father. Sin makes us miserable, but Christ was without sin.
3. He trusted his Father and submitted to his will. The Father desired joyful obedience, not just obedience, from Christ. Hence, Jesus journeyed to the most terrifying place in the world, the cross, with joy set before him (Heb. 12:2).
4. He knew that his faithfulness, even in the most difficult circumstances (e.g., his temptation, Matt. 4:1–11),

would lead to his glory and the salvation of his people. How could that not make him joyful even when he was weeping?

5. He claimed to be joyful. In Luke 10:21, Jesus "rejoiced in the Holy Spirit" because the Father had revealed to "little children" the salvation that comes through his victory over the Devil (Luke 10:18–20; Heb. 2:14).

6. He loved his friends, such as John, who would have brought him joy.

7. He had a peculiar knowledge of the attributes of God, the fountain of blessedness, which meant that he was assured of the same for himself personally and for his people corporately.

If there were ever a place to excuse Christ for lacking joy, it would be Golgotha. Yet as Spurgeon wonderfully observes,

> A great sorrow was on Christ when our load was laid on him; but a greater joy flashed into his mind when he thought that we were thus recovered from our lost estate. . . . Even "Eloi, Eloi, lama sabachthani?" ["My God, my God, why have you forsaken me?"], when the depths of its woe have been sounded, will be found to have pearls of joy in its caverns.[5]

Because of his work on our behalf, Christ knew that we would experience joy. God would, through Christ and the Spirit, offer us continual fresh communications from the fullness of his blessed being. Thus we have hope that we will drink from the "rivers of pleasure" and shall refresh ourselves "in the eternal springs of life, light, and joy forevermore."[6] But here exists the glory of our redemption, which begins in this life, not in the life to come: "Though you have not seen him, you love him. Though you do not now see him, you believe in him and rejoice with joy that is inexpressible and filled with glory, obtaining the outcome of your faith, the salvation of your souls" (1 Pet. 1:8).

Application

Since God is the fountain of all blessedness, we cannot be truly happy in this life until he becomes our God. We are only as happy or miserable as the god we serve. Nothing can offer more happiness than what it rightly possesses in itself. God is infinite in happiness and so supplies joy and satisfaction first (and preeminently) to his Son and then, by virtue of our union with him and the indwelling Spirit, to us.

George Swinnock wisely states,

> Those who serve the flesh as their god are miserable (Rom. 16:18; Phil. 3:18) because their god is vile, weak, deceitful, and transitory (Pss. 49:20; 73:25; Isa. 31:3; Jer. 17:9). Similarly, those who prize the world as their god are miserable because their god is vain, troublesome, uncertain, and fleeting (Eccl. 1:2–3; 5:10; 1 Cor. 7:29–31; 1 Tim. 6:9–10). But those who have an interest in this great God are happy: "Happy is that people, whose God is the LORD" (Ps. 144:15).[7]

[As Christ received his happiness from God through the Spirit, so we get happiness from him in the same way.] That is the only joy worth having, because it comes from an inexhaustible fountain overflowing into our hearts, a joy that will be increased in heaven for all eternity.

The highest and greatest gift that God can give us is not riches, prestige, life, or even salvation itself. No, the greatest gift is himself, of which no greater gift exists. The blessed triune God is ours because he gave himself to us through the Father, Son, and Holy Spirit. Indeed,

> The LORD is my chosen portion and my cup;
>   you hold my lot.
> The lines have fallen for me in pleasant places;
>   indeed, I have a beautiful inheritance. (Ps. 16:5–6)

Finally, when you are carrying your various crosses in this

life, remember Jesus. Remember his joy, and claim it as your own, for in him and by the Spirit, his joy really becomes yours. This precious gift will often carry the aroma of patience and endurance, but it still remains joy because of the reward that awaits us (1 Pet. 1:6–9).

13

GOD IS GLORIOUS

Blessed be his glorious name forever;
    may the whole earth be filled with his glory!
Amen and Amen!

Psalm 72:19

Doctrine

There are basically two ways that we can speak of God's glory, a term that denotes his divine splendor and the magnificence for which he is worthy of honor. First, God's essential glory represents the sum of his attributes, which together make him the "God of glory" (Acts 7:2). His glory, as Thomas Watson notes, is the "sparkling of the Deity."[1] God's life lies in his glory, and it cannot increase or decrease, since it is already infinite, unchangeable, and eternal. This glory belongs to the Father, Son, and Holy Spirit, because each person shares in the divine essence. Second, there is a glory ascribed to God in terms of what his creatures bring to him (1 Chron. 16:29). This latter glory has in view our praise, worship, obedience, and delight as we keep the name of the Lord holy in all that we do (Matt. 6:9).

The Scriptures speak of God's glory usually in reference to something he has done (see 1 Chron. 29:12–13; Ps. 72:18–19). All that he does is glorious because it manifests his glorious nature. As

103

the sum of all his attributes, this glorious "sparkling" remains too much for us to bear. Moses wanted to see God's glory (Ex. 33:18), but God made clear that that was impossible: "You cannot see my face, for man shall not see me and live" (v. 20). Even apart from sin, we could not withstand God's naked revealed glory. Yet sin exacerbates the problem intensely.

God—and thus also his glory—remains incomprehensible to us. He condescends to give us a little taste of his glory, because he freely chooses, in his glory, to reveal himself to us. We must firmly keep in mind that God has set his glory as the goal of all things, not only in relation to how his creatures must and will act but also in relation to himself. He cannot give his glory to another (Isa. 48:11), but he can and must glorify himself. The three persons in the Godhead all delight to glorify each other, eternally and lovingly.

Our aim is no different: "So, whether you eat or drink, or whatever you do, do all to the glory of God" (1 Cor. 10:31). We glorify the Father who gave us life, the Son who gave his life for us, and the Spirit who produces new life in us. We give God the glory due his name (1 Chron. 16:29).

Yet when we glorify God, we add nothing to his essential glory, the glory he already possesses in himself. We glorify God only as we give him the honor due him in this world according to the way he has dictated in his Word.

The Glory of the God-Man and His Bride

We behold the glory of God in the person of Jesus Christ (2 Cor. 3:18; 4:6) not only in this life but also in the one to come. Christ has three distinct glories, all of which we must examine for the improvement of our faith. First, Christ, because he is God, possesses an *essential glory* inherent to himself, as just discussed above. But Christ also has two other glories that we must comprehend.

Second, Christ possesses a *personal glory*. Jesus has a peculiar glory belonging to him alone. Even the Father and the Spirit do not possess this specific glory, for neither are fully God and fully man. In this manner, Christ is the God-man, what theologians call a *complex person* or *composite person*. Thus, we speak of him possessing a distinct personal glory.

The union of the divine and human natures in Christ leads Thomas Goodwin to describe such glory as "the highest manifestation of the Godhead that could have been communicated to creatures."[2] As a result, "more of God's glory shall instantly shine forth in . . . the man, Christ Jesus, having the God-head dwelling in him personally, than by God's making millions of worlds . . . furnished with glories."[3] That is, Christ makes the glory of God not only possible but also visible. The Puritan John Arrowsmith notes that just as God is invisible, his glory would be "too dazzling for our weak eyes." As we cannot behold the sun in its sphere, we can nevertheless behold the sun in a basin of water. Christ is the "basin" that enables us to behold God's glory.[4]

If we cannot behold the attributes of God directly, how can we understand Isaiah's apparent sight of God in the fullness of his glory (Isa. 6:1–7)? Did Isaiah not gaze on the holiness of Yahweh ("Holy, holy, holy is the Lord of hosts; the whole earth is full of his glory!" Isa. 6:3)? Isaiah did not in fact see God directly (and live) but instead saw Christ. This is precisely how the apostle John interprets Isaiah's experience: "Isaiah said these things because he saw his glory and spoke of him" (John 12:41; see also Acts 7:55–56).

Isaiah saw God's glory in the person of Christ, not God's glory that he experiences in himself (see John 1:18). Isaiah saw what was fitting for him as a sinner (Isa. 6:5). Like Isaiah, we can be thankful that we see God's glory in the person of Christ, because that glory, when beheld by faith, saves rather than consumes us.

Third, Christ possesses a *mediatorial glory*, one, according to Thomas Goodwin, "acquired, purchased, and merited" by his work (in obedience to the Father) on behalf of sinners.[5] We may call this a *superadded* glory involving Christ's people as his bride.

And the bride of Christ is, naturally, his glory, just as a woman is the glory of man (1 Cor. 11:7). We, who are his body, are "the fullness of him who fills all in all" (Eph. 1:23).

As the bride of Christ receives the blessings of his work on their behalf, Christ receives glory as the fruit of his labor. The more blessings he pours out from heaven as the resurrected King of glory, the more he gets glory. In fact, the more love Christ shows to the church, the more love he shows to himself. For the man who loves his wife loves himself (Eph. 5:28). Thus, in his bride Christ is glorified: "As for Titus, he is my partner and fellow worker for your benefit. And as for our brothers, they are messengers of the churches, the glory of Christ" (2 Cor. 8:23). Jesus prayed, "All mine are yours, and yours are mine, and I am glorified in them" (John 17:10).

Since God's great end is the glory of his Son (Col. 1:16), Christ must necessarily be glorified in those for whom he died. He makes the church pure, beautiful, and holy, which means that the "Lord Christ is, and will be, glorious unto all eternity."[6]

As John Piper has coined the phrase "God is most glorified in us when we are most satisfied in him,"[7] I would like to add (by way of complement) that "God is most satisfied in himself when Christ is most glorified in us." In other words, in God's purposes for his Son, the world, and his people, God is "most satisfied" when we as his children give the most glory to his Son.

Application

Each of the glories described above has relevance for us. All that God is has relevance for us. If who God is has no relevance for us, then we have a problem with our conception of God.

First, in terms of God's essential glory, we are confronted with the fact that God remains too great for us. His majesty, holiness, power, and knowledge are utterly beyond our comprehension. Far from causing despair, this truth should comfort us. We do not need a god we can manage but one utterly beyond our ability to comprehend.

Second, Christ's personal glory has a bearing on our lives. Because of God's essential glory and his desire to have communion with his creatures, he condescends in the person of Christ. Christ's personal glory is the primary way we come to know, love, and enjoy God. Only through the God-man can we have any access to, sight of, knowledge of, and enjoyment of God. Christ makes theology, worship, communion, and heaven on earth possible. Apart from him, we as sinners have no hope of a relationship with God.

Third, Christ's mediatorial glory remains applicable to us. The prospect of the beatific vision, whereby we shall be like him because we shall see him (face-to-face) as he is (1 John 3:2), stirs our faith, hope, and love in this life. Such anticipation enables us to bring glory to Christ on earth as his bride. Our desire to be holy and to refrain from sin has as its primary goal not our personal happiness, however important that may be, but the glory of Christ. Our chief business on earth is to glorify the Ever-Glorious One.

14

GOD IS MAJESTIC

Yours, O LORD, is the greatness and the power and
the glory and the victory and the majesty, for all that
is in the heavens and in the earth is yours. Yours is
the kingdom, O LORD, and you are exalted as head
above all.

1 Chronicles 29:11

Doctrine

[God's majesty—also understood as his dominion or eminence and
often paired with his glory in treatments on the divine attributes—
is as essential to his being as his love, power, or eternity.] If he does
not possess dominion or majesty, he is not God. Because God has
infinite power, eternal goodness, and unchangeable omniscience,
he must necessarily be supremely majestic. In God's Word, we
find not a few isolated references to the dominion and majesty of
God but rather a multitude of vivid descriptions that highlight his
greatness in memorable ways.

King David's prayer of praise and supplication in the public
assembly of God's people recognizes God for who he really is, the
Majestic One: "Yours, O LORD, is the greatness and the power
and the glory and the victory and the majesty, for all that is in the

heavens and in the earth is yours. Yours is the kingdom, O LORD, and you are exalted as head above all" (1 Chron. 29:11).

Here David speaks of God's majesty by referring to his power and glory. He then describes why he is majestic, namely, because "all that is in the heavens and in the earth" is his. God does not simply want his people to affirm his majesty, but rather he wants them to understand why he is majestic. The *why* remains as important as the *what* when we speak of his attributes. His dominion is the reason for his majesty.

God's attributes, especially his majesty, should in some sense cause great fear and awe among his people. Job chastises his friends for misunderstanding God: "Will not his majesty terrify you, and the dread of him fall upon you?" (Job 13:11). Here Job connects God's majesty with our response to it. Later in the book, Elihu grasps this appropriate reverence:

> Out of the north comes golden splendor;
>> God is clothed with awesome majesty.
> The Almighty—we cannot find him;
>> he is great in power;
>> justice and abundant righteousness he will not violate.
> Therefore men fear him;
>> he does not regard any who are wise in their own conceit.
>> (Job 37:22–24)

God's majesty should strike a holy fear into the hearts and minds of God's people. Why? Because we know that his majesty is his power is his justice is his dominion. The majestic God cannot dwell with or tolerate the proud, and his dominion over them means he can and will judge them. Thus God challenges Job to act like God:

> Adorn yourself with majesty and dignity;
>> clothe yourself with glory and splendor.
> Pour out the overflowings of your anger,
>> and look on everyone who is proud and abase him.

Look on everyone who is proud and bring him low
    and tread down the wicked where they stand.
Hide them all in the dust together;
    bind their faces in the world below.
Then will I also acknowledge to you
    that your own right hand can save you. (Job 40:10–14)

Of course, Job cannot do this, but God can. He does not merely judge the proud; he majestically judges them in his dominion over them. He shows the vast difference between himself and them. He challenges Job to perform that which is impossible. God highlights his majesty by the fact that he alone is clothed with "glory and splendor." The psalmist praises God: "O LORD my God, you are very great! You are clothed with splendor and majesty, covering yourself with light as with a garment, stretching out the heavens like a tent" (Ps. 104:1–2). When Job does what God (alone) can do, then Job may compare himself with the Majestic One.

We make a distinction between his dominion and power insofar as the latter refers to his ability to effect his will, whereas the former speaks of his royal (majestic) prerogative to do whatever he pleases. We understand God's physical power as his omnipotence and his moral power as his dominion or lordship.

In exercising his sovereign power, he brings all creatures into subjection to himself. In exercising his dominion, he possesses a sovereign right to subdue them. Because we make no distinction, properly speaking, between the attributes in God, we cannot comprehend the dominion of God unless we consider all his attributes within the perfection of that dominion. For example, we viewed God's dominion in the context of his judgment on the proud. Likewise, his is a righteous, powerful, and eternal dominion. Charnock sees inseparable union between power and dominion: "It is as possible for him not to be God as not to be supreme. . . . To fancy an infinite power without a supreme dominion, is to fancy a mighty senseless statue, fit to be beheld, but not fit to be obeyed."[1]

Unlike men, who derive their dominion from God (Gen. 1:26;

Rom. 13:1), God's dominion is completely independent. His independence makes his dominion absolute, or reflective of unlimited authority. As he exercises his dominion, his other attributes (e.g., wisdom, righteousness, and goodness) are all present, which means that his dominion cannot be tyrannical, oppressive, or unmerciful but is perfectly good, just, and wise.

Some believe that by the act of creation, God limited his own dominion in favor of the free choice of humans and angels. This remains impossible, since God's dominion necessarily unites with all his attributes. He cannot relinquish one attribute, such as dominion, without relinquishing all his attributes, which is ontologically impossible. The majesty of God's dominion comes from his naked unlimited power clad in the beauty of his holy, eternal, unchangeable being. Consequently, his dominion over his creatures must necessarily be forever. By ontological necessity, man remains under the rule of God.

God's Majesty in Christ

For the sake of his name and the glory of Christ, God exercises his dominion both in subduing rebellious sinners and in making them love him. Some believe and others do not because God in his dominion decreed it. Thus, God the Father ordained that Christ should die for those sinners appointed to salvation and that the Holy Spirit should apply such to those for whom Christ died (1 Pet. 1:1–2).

The exaltation of Christ displays God's dominion. Christ received comprehensive authority (Matt. 28:18; John 5:22; Eph. 1:22; Rev. 3:21), according to the pleasure and will of God, from the one free to give such authority by virtue of his dominion. The act of giving or rewarding testifies to the dominion of the person who grants (Heb. 11:6). Thus we can distinguish between God's essential dominion and the economical dominion belonging to Christ.

For Christians, we are to principally understand God's dominion in terms of the dominion given to the Son. Psalm 45 speaks of such dominion. The psalmist first describes Christ as the one whom God has blessed forever (v. 2) and then addresses the glory and dominion of the King, the coming Messiah, Jesus Christ:

> Gird your sword on your thigh, O mighty one,
> > in your splendor and majesty!
>
> In your majesty ride out victoriously
> > for the cause of truth and meekness and righteousness;
> > let your right hand teach you awesome deeds!
> Your arrows are sharp
> > in the heart of the king's enemies;
> > the peoples fall under you.
>
> Your throne, O God, is forever and ever.
> > The scepter of your kingdom is a scepter of uprightness;
> > you have loved righteousness and hated wickedness.
> Therefore God, your God, has anointed you
> > with the oil of gladness beyond your companions;
> > your robes are all fragrant with myrrh and aloes and cassia.
> > > (Ps. 45:3–8)

What makes Christ majestic? His gracious speech (v. 2), military power (vv. 3–5), eternal throne (v. 6), Spirit-anointed moral holiness (v. 7), and adored position (vv. 8–9) do so. God has given him the name that is above every name (Phil. 2:9). Thus, he can command his disciples to bless the nations, because all authority in heaven and on earth has been given to him (Matt. 28:18). As the receiver of the Holy Spirit (Acts 2:33), Christ can subdue the hearts of sinners, a work more powerful and majestic than creating a thousand worlds of loving creatures.

When the officers came to arrest Christ, they were unsuccessful. Why? In part because, as they recognized, "no one ever spoke like this man!" (John 7:46). In Christ's words was a majesty that confounded his enemies to the point that he caused them to fall back: "When Jesus said to them, 'I am he,' they drew back and fell to the ground" (John 18:6). These words of Christ connect to Psalm 9:3, "When my enemies turn back, they stumble and perish before your presence."

Peter was an eyewitness of Christ's majesty: "But we were eyewitnesses of his majesty. For when he received honor and glory from God the Father, and the voice was borne to him by the Majestic Glory, 'This is my beloved Son, with whom I am well pleased'" (2 Pet. 1:16–17), Peter tasted what we shall one day experience from God through his Son. In other words, we shall experience God's majesty in Christ one day by sight, just as Peter did but in a better way, because we will sinlessly and ceaselessly gaze on that majesty for all eternity.

Application

As we contemplate the one clothed with majesty (Ps. 93:1), we must be filled with awe—indeed, a submissive awe. When we worship, we must do so with "reverence and awe" (Heb. 12:28). In the Christian life, God does not settle for second place. Sometimes we may intellectually assent that he should be first, while our actions betray our true theological convictions, which lack the awe God deserves. We must prefer God above all things, because he is above all things. His majesty demands such reverential preference.

When we consider the infinite demerit of our sin against an infinitely majestic God, we should be totally humbled that we are utterly unable to remedy this problem in ourselves. We cannot make satisfaction or restitution for the smallest sin we have committed against such a God. Calvin beautifully expresses the humility that should come over us when we consider God's majesty:

> Hence that dread and wonder with which Scripture commonly represents the saints as stricken and overcome whenever they felt the presence of God. Thus it comes about that we see men who in his absence normally remained firm and constant, but who,

when he manifests his glory, are so shaken and struck dumb as to be laid low by the dread of death—are in fact overwhelmed by it and almost annihilated. As a consequence, we must infer that man is never sufficiently touched and affected by the awareness of his lowly state until he has compared himself with God's majesty.[2]

Anselm famously affirmed concerning God, "We believe that thou art a being than which nothing greater can be conceived."[3] Such remains true not only in regard to God's majesty but also in regard to his works toward us in Christ. God does such majestic works through his Son that none greater can be conceived. His majesty is stamped all over his works of redemption through Christ, the God-man.

Through the necessary path of humiliation, Christ arrived at the place of glory and honor (Heb. 2:9). We too come to the place of glory and honor through the path of suffering. We share in Christ's majesty as the King of kings. We are "more than conquerors" (Rom. 8:37). Thus, our faith leads us to hope in our future reward of being crowned with glory and honor in Christ's kingdom.

When God challenged Job to adorn himself with majesty, he absolutely could not rise to the occasion. But when God grants to us the gift of his Son, we are then blessed with a share in Christ's majesty. What is impossible with man is possible with God.

15

GOD IS SOVEREIGN

For from him and through him and to him are all
things. To him be glory forever. Amen.

Romans 11:36

Doctrine

Everything that happens in the universe derives from God's will.
This truth causes us to praise him:

> Worthy are you, our Lord and God,
>   to receive glory and honor and power,
> for you created all things,
>   and by your will they existed and were created. (Rev. 4:11)

The triune God has one will. Love between the three divine
persons is an act of God's singular, eternal will. The Father, Son,
and Spirit must love each other because they share the same will.
God wills his own goodness and holiness naturally and necessarily, which is why we refer to this as God's necessary will.

We can also speak of God's internal works or activity, which
we can describe in the following manner:

1. God's will is independent: he wills of himself and is in-
   duced by no one to will whatever he wills.

2. God's will consists of one indivisible act: because his simplicity and his will are identical with his essence, God's will cannot be split into different acts or aspects.

God also freely wills and determines all things. In connection with his free will, Francis Turretin says, "God wills all created things not to make himself perfect (as if he stood in need of them), but to communicate himself and to manifest his goodness and glory in them. Hence because he could be without them without any detriment to his happiness, he is said to will them freely."[1]

The outward works of God relate to his free will by which he creates, sustains, and relates to the created order. If God does not order all things, then he has given up his responsibility to us and to himself. Both are impossibilities. Of course, many have questioned God's goodness based on their apprehension of how God is "doing things." However, we must keep in mind that God is utterly incomprehensible and that we are all in a far more precarious state if God is not in fact working all things together after the counsel of his will (Eph. 1:11).

We can also speak of God's will in terms of his sovereignty and his providence. The eternal God ordains all things from eternity and brings them to their intended goal in history, to the praise of his name. God "works all things according to the counsel of his will" (Eph. 1:11). Nebuchadnezzar recognized this reality, attributing to God the proper glory and honor due to him because of the extensiveness and power of his will:

I blessed the Most High, and praised and honored him who lives forever,

for his dominion is an everlasting dominion,
and his kingdom endures from generation to
generation;
all the inhabitants of the earth are accounted as nothing,

> and he does according to his will among the host of
>   heaven
> and among the inhabitants of the earth;
>   and none can stay his hand
>   or say to him, "What have you done?"
>   (Dan. 4:34–35)

The Scriptures do not hide the absolute sovereignty of God: "Our God is in the heavens; he does all that he pleases" (Ps. 115:3).

Everything depends on God as the Primary Cause both of its substance and its circumstances (Isa. 45:7; Lam. 3:37–38). He often works through means, despite not needing them to accomplish his ends. His providence both preserves (Ps. 104:19–20; Acts 17:28; Heb. 1:3) and governs all things (Gen. 50:20; Ps. 29:10).[2]

Providence is part of God's will but should not be confused with his predestination or eternal decree. Rather, providence involves God's execution of that decree within the time and space of his creation. We can see this thinking clearly in three descriptions of God's providence. William Pemble speaks of it as

> an external and temporal action of God, whereby he preserves, governs, and disposes all and singular things, which are, and are done, both the creatures, and the faculties and actions of the creatures, and directs them both to the mediate ends, and to the last end of all, after a set and determinate manner, according to the most free decree, and counsel of his own will; that himself in all things may be glorified.[3]

John Owen refers to God's providence as an

> ineffable act or work of Almighty God, whereby he cherishes, sustains, and governs the world, or all things by him created, moving them, agreeably to those natures which he endowed them withal in the beginning, unto those ends which he has proposed.[4]

Likewise, the *Synopsis of Purer Theology* (1625), a concise treatise of seventeenth-century Dutch Reformed theology, calls God's providence the

> pre-existent structural ordaining in God's mind, of things toward a goal; that is, the practical knowledge of God whereby He pre-ordained each and every single thing from eternity and directs them to their proper goal—for his own glory.[5]

Several elements are present in these definitions of providence. Put simply, God governs all things toward a goal, namely, his glory. We can thank God that we worship him, because he has determined both that we do so and that we stand in awe of his holy being as image bearers of the true and living God.

Obadiah Sedgwick helpfully connects God's providence to his other attributes: "Divine providence is an external action of God whereby He conserves and governs all things wisely, holily, justly, and powerfully, to the admiration of His own glory."[6] Thus, when speaking of his providence and the manner in which he governs all things, we must always keep in mind all his attributes. In this way, we may appreciate the manner in which he governs all things, not just the fact that he does.

God's government of the world is just that: God's government. He cannot rule in any other way than what is consistent with his being. He necessarily governs justly and wisely as the sovereign Lord who exercises his rule in the most beautiful manner.

God's Sovereignty in Christ's Death

The permission of sin belongs to God and is never a bare permission of his sovereign will. As the Leiden professors argue in the *Synopsis of Purer Theology,*

> For although sins are evil, and accordingly cannot be provided by God, nevertheless the permission of them is good. So then, God both wills and directly decrees the permission, and ordains it for some good purpose that is greater than that of which the absence

is the evil that is permitted. For since God is good to the highest degree, He would in no way permit there to be anything evil in his workings, unless He were not so almighty that even concerning evil He would still do good, as Augustine justly states.[7]

We might think that permission makes God out to be merely an interested spectator who sits in a watchtower instead of working all things according to his will. But when God permits an evil act, he does so not passively but actively. God's permission of evil thus involves an indirect act of God's will.

The death of Christ highlights this truth in a most striking manner. As Peter underscores in his sermon to his Jewish hearers at Pentecost, the providence of God involves the permission of evil men killing Christ:

> Men of Israel, hear these words: Jesus of Nazareth, a man attested to you by God with mighty works and wonders and signs that God did through him in your midst, as you yourselves know—this Jesus, delivered up according to the definite plan and foreknowledge of God, you crucified and killed by the hands of lawless men. (Acts 2:22–23)

Similarly, the believers in Acts 4 also pray with these truths in mind: "For truly in this city there were gathered together against your holy servant Jesus, whom you anointed, both Herod and Pontius Pilate, along with the Gentiles and the peoples of Israel, to do whatever your hand and your plan had predestined to take place" (Acts 4:27–28).

God's permission of evil men murdering the Holy and Righteous One (Acts 3:14) is not opposed to his secret will. At the same time, God rightly holds such men responsible for putting Christ on the cross. How the sovereign purpose of God and the heinous actions of men in crucifying Christ work together, we cannot fully understand. This much we do know: the Bible reveals both concepts (in one verse in Acts 2:23!); God ordained Christ's death, and evil men killed him. In accordance with his will, God in the end powerfully and righteously brings to pass events that glorify himself. Nowhere is this truth more obvious than in the death of his Son.

Before Christ died, he predicted his death: "And he began to teach them that the Son of Man must suffer many things and be rejected by the elders and the chief priests and the scribes and be killed, and after three days rise again" (Mark 8:31). Christ understood his mission and life from the prophetic Old Testament Scriptures so clearly that he knew with absolute certainty what would happen to him. God leaves nothing to chance, "declaring the end from the beginning and from ancient times things not yet done, saying, 'My counsel shall stand, and I will accomplish all my purpose'" (Isa. 46:10).

Whether working through ordinary means, such as the provision of food, rain, and clothing (Pss. 136:25; 147:8–9; Matt. 6:30, 32), or working out our salvation according to his plan in Christ Jesus, God will accomplish his purposes as the sovereign Lord.

Application[8]

If God does not exercise sovereignty over all events and actions of his creatures, as well as over all creation, then we are in a precarious position indeed. Christ found comfort in his shameful death on the cross, because he was fulfilling the glorious purposes of his Father to redeem mankind from sin and misery. We cannot afford to be tentative about the providence of God in those horrible events. Rather, for Christ, as well as for us, nothing could be more certain than that he entered this world to fulfill, in the most striking detail, all that was written of him in the Old Testament. For example, God said that not one of his bones would be broken (Ps. 34:20), and thus his bones were not broken: "For these things took place that the Scripture might be fulfilled: 'Not one of his bones will be broken'" (John 19:36).

In our own lives, we ought to believe with all our hearts in the sovereignty of God over all things. His will comforts us in times of trouble because nothing can happen outside the decree of our good God. Our Father in heaven truly works all things together for our good (Rom. 8:28), a promise that gives us comfort only if we affirm his sovereignty.

Why do good things happen to bad people, and why do bad things happen to good people? Strictly speaking, there has only ever been one good person who had bad things happen to him: Christ. Amazingly, he even volunteered to be ill-treated and scorned by humanity. But the Scriptures are filled with examples of good things happening to bad people (Ps. 73:3; Mal. 3:15), as well as some really bad things happening to "good" people (e.g., Joseph, Daniel; cf. Ps. 44:22).

The brilliant fourteenth-century archbishop of Canterbury Thomas Bradwardine tells a story in his *De causa Dei contra Pelagium* that can help us understand this delicate theological problem and can offer some hope to those who have suffered a great deal in their Christian lives:

> Once upon a time there was a hermit who was thinking that the wicked received the good and the righteous received evil. He began to doubt the existence of a good God. He gave up his solitary life and wandered through the world. While doing this, an angel, in the form of a man, joined him.
>
> First, together they met somebody who met them politely and treated them very well with accommodation.
>
> Rising at midnight the angel took a golden cup from the host and went away with the hermit.
>
> Second, they stayed with someone else who equally treated them well. Rising at midnight with the hermit the angel went to the cradle and strangled the baby.
>
> Third, they met someone who did not let them stay in his home, but rather outside. In the morning the angel knocked on the door and gave the wicked man a golden cup, which he had stolen from the first good man they had stayed with.

123

Fourth, they came to a man who treated them most kindly. When the angel and hermit were about to leave, the angel asked the host to send his servant with them to show them the way to go. When they reached a bridge over the rapid waters, the angel threw the servant into the river.

The hermit wanted to leave this apparently wicked angel.

But the angel told the hermit to wait and listen how everything happened according to God's just order: The angel was an angel of God to teach the hermit that many things that seem unjust to humans are very good.

The first man they met whom they took the cup from profited because, before possessing the cup, he feared God. But after getting the cup he became drunk every day with that cup. God sent the angel to remove this incentive to drunkenness in order that the man be saved.

To the third man whom I gave the golden cup, that is, the wicked man who did not give hospitality, the angel did much harm to him, even though he appeared to outwardly prosper. This man became a drunk once in possession of the cup. God gave him the cup as a sign of judgment, even though he thought he prospered.

Regarding the man whose child I killed, he was generous to the poor before he had his son. But after having a son he no longer treated the poor or cared for them. God ordered that the angel kill the child so that the man would no longer endanger his eternal salvation and return to his previous life of generosity.

Regarding the servant whom the angel threw over into the rushing waters, that servant was about to murder his kind master and his family, including his wife and child, that night. But the Lord loved this family and so prevented that evil.

Then the angel said: "Off you go and stop judging divine providence in the wrong way, because you see bad things happen to good people and good things to bad people."[9]

God's providence remains the work of an infinitely wise,

good, and powerful God. Even when we cannot understand all the details of each story, we can nevertheless cast ourselves on the one who cannot act in a way contrary to who he is. And who he is gives us all the comfort we ultimately need in a world full of perplexing trials.

16

GOD IS LOVE

Anyone who does not love does not know God, because God is love.

1 John 4:8

Doctrine

God is love. The Bible plainly declares that to us—not just in the explicit words of 1 John 4:8 ("God is love") but also in literally thousands of ways throughout God's Word. As J. I. Packer says, "To know God's love is indeed heaven on earth."[1]

If there were no world and no universe, the persons of the Trinity would still have an infinite, blessed, unchangeable, eternal, powerful love between them—an inward love. This love satisfies them because it is a perfect love; it cannot be increased or decreased in any way. Yet according to the free decision of God to extend his love outward, others may be objects of it as well.

God loves Jesus, all creatures, human beings, the elect, and the goodness in the elect. His love is best described as an *affection*, a love that arises inwardly and extends outward. His love is not a *passion*, as if something causes God to love. His love to others is caused by himself. If someone is pleasing to God, it is because God has made that person pleasing to himself according to his love and grace.

God exists as an inexhaustible fountain of love. His goal for his creatures is that they love God and one another, for we are never more like him than when we love. Heaven itself will forever be a place of love (1 Cor. 13:13).

There are different ways of understanding God's love. While his intra-Trinitarian love is eternal and therefore natural and necessary, God loves his creatures voluntarily, not necessarily. According to this outward, voluntary impulse, we can identify a threefold distinction in God's love:

1. God's universal love toward all things: "The LORD is good to all, and his mercy is over all that he has made" (Ps. 145:9). Even the creatures of the earth are beneficiaries of God's love.

2. God's love toward all human beings, both elect and reprobate: "But I say to you, Love your enemies and pray for those who persecute you, so that you may be sons of your Father who is in heaven. For he makes his sun rise on the evil and on the good, and sends rain on the just and on the unjust" (Matt. 5:44–45). God still loves a person who hates and rejects him, even granting him the ability to manifest such hate in thoughts, words, and actions.

3. God's special love toward his people: "But you are a chosen race, a royal priesthood, a holy nation, a people for his own possession, that you may proclaim the excellencies of him who called you out of darkness into his marvelous light" (1 Pet. 2:9). This theme dominates the pages of Scripture, compared with the other types of love that God shows toward his creation and unbelievers.

Thus in the Old Testament, God declares through the prophet Isaiah,

"For the mountains may depart
 and the hills be removed,

but my steadfast love shall not depart from you,
    and my covenant of peace shall not be removed,"
says the LORD, who has compassion on you. (Isa. 54:10)

Likewise, the New Testament proclaims, "For I am sure that neither death nor life, nor angels nor rulers, nor things present nor things to come, nor powers, nor height nor depth, nor anything else in all creation, will be able to separate us from the love of God in Christ Jesus our Lord" (Rom. 8:38–39).

The third category of love—God's love toward his people—has as its special focus the love that God shows to us in and through Christ Jesus. Here we may speak of a further threefold type of love:

1. God's love of benevolence, understood in terms of his election and predestination: ". . . even as he chose us in him before the foundation of the world, that we should be holy and blameless before him. In love he predestined us for adoption to himself as sons through Jesus Christ, according to the purpose of his will, to the praise of his glorious grace, with which he has blessed us in the Beloved" (Eph. 1:4–6).

2. God's love of beneficence, whereby he wills to redeem his people: "He who did not spare his own Son but gave him up for us all, how will he not also with him graciously give us all things?" (Rom. 8:32).

3. God's love of delight or friendship, whereby he rewards his people according to their holiness: "Whoever has my commandments and keeps them, he it is who loves me. And he who loves me will be loved by my Father, and I will love him and manifest myself to him" (John 14:21; see also v. 23).

God is good in himself and so delights in himself. For example, he delights in his infinite, eternal, unchangeable, powerful, abundant, and majestic goodness. This delight in his essence provides the basis for his enjoyment of his creatures. If God loves himself, he must love the image of his own goodness when it is in others. In loving others, God loves himself and his own virtues. God loves all things according to the degree of loveliness in it, which loveliness comes from him, according to the wisdom of his purposes and grace.

God's Love for Christ

We can understand God's outward love toward others by focusing on his love for his Son. So, for example, the Son of God exists as the special object of the Father's delight and love. Christ's beauty cannot be compared to any created person. While truly referring to Israel's king, Psalm 45 is ultimately fulfilled in Christ: "You are the most handsome of the sons of men; grace is poured upon your lips; therefore God has blessed you forever" (v. 2).

Even before the incarnation, the Father speaks of the prospect of his servant, the Messiah: "Behold my servant, whom I uphold, my chosen, in whom my soul delights" (Isa. 42:1). The Father's delight is renewed after the incarnation at Christ's baptism (Matt. 3:17) and transfiguration (Matt. 17:5).

At Christ's baptism, the Father speaks to Christ of his love for him: first, for Christ (to personally assure him), and second, for us (that we may know how much the Father loves the Son).

As Christ testifies, "The Father loves the Son and has given all things into his hand" (John 3:35; see also John 5:20). Not only the Father but also Jesus himself desires and prays that believers may know of the love the Father has for the Son (John 17:23, 26). God reveals this intra-Trinitarian love so we might realize that in loving the Son, the Father also loves us. To highlight this love of God for his people, Calvin quotes Augustine as follows:

> God's love . . . is incomprehensible and unchangeable. For it was not after we were reconciled to him through the blood of his Son that he began to love us. Rather, he has loved us before

the world was created, that we also might be his sons along with his only-begotten Son—before we became anything at all. The fact that we were reconciled through Christ's death must not be understood as if his Son reconciled us to him that he might now begin to love those whom he had hated. Rather, we have already been reconciled to him who loves us, with whom we were enemies on account of sin. The apostle will testify whether I am speaking the truth: "God shows his love for us in that while we were yet sinners Christ died for us" [Rom. 5:8]. Therefore, he loved us even when we practiced enmity toward him and committed wickedness. Thus in a marvelous and divine way he loved us even when he hated us. For he hated us for what we were that he had not made; yet because our wickedness had not entirely consumed his handiwork, he knew how, at the same time, to hate in each one of us what we had made, and to love what he had made.[2]

The gift of his Son remains the greatest gift God can give (Rom. 8:32). In one sense, the only truth we need to believe concerning his love is that he gave his Son for us. Nothing is more glorious or shows his love better. Nothing causes us to raise our thoughts and hearts so high as recognizing that God sent his Son to die a cursed death so that we might know the love of God.

According to William Bates, "A greater love was expressed to wretched man, than to Christ himself."[3] How so? "God in giving him to die for us, declared that our salvation was more dear to him than the life of his only Son."[4] In other words, God would never have put his Son through such torment and suffering unless he wished to display the greatness of his love toward his people. Every humiliation, trial, heartache, and suffering that our Savior experienced was God showing his love toward us.

Not only God's love but also the Savior's love comes to its highest expression in Christ's death for us. His love was

so pure and great, there can be no resemblance, much less any parallel of it; for he was perfectly holy, and so the privilege of immortality was due to him; and his life was infinitely more precious than the lives of angels and men; yet he laid it down, and submitted to a cursed death, and to that which was infinitely more bitter, the wrath of God: and all this for sinful men, who were under the just and heavy displeasure of the Almighty.[5]

Application

God's love for us in Christ has many practical applications for the Christian life. We know that the "love of Christ controls us" (2 Cor. 5:14) because he died for us. Do we love God with the type of love that we ought to? In preaching a sermon on Exodus 3:14, titled "I Am That I Am," the Church of Scotland minister John Love complained,

> But, from experience, it is plain, how cold, how dead, how perverse, the hearts of men are, as to the great truths concerning the being and perfections of God. And it is only because these fundamental truths are basely and carelessly passed over by many preachers, that the hearts of many professors of religion do not fret, and boil, and foam with indignation, in the hearing of the word of God. I am persuaded that if the glory of the true God were faithfully, and in its proper majesty, published as it hath sometimes been, unless God should sovereignly change the hearts of many, it would soon thin many places of worship. Were God to appear in the sanctuary, as he hath sometimes done, the whole herd of hollow-hearted, worldly, conceited professors, would flee from him, as wild beasts keep at a distance from a fire blazing in the desert.[6]

We must meditate carefully on this attribute of God because our own attitude toward others will change when we come to grasp God's love for us. In other words, if God and Christ can set their hearts on hell-deserving sinners, who by nature hate God, then how can we have a different attitude than God toward the same people? We love unbelievers with a love that seeks to win them, not only by words but also by deeds, to the love of God in Christ.

We love believers because, after we have loved God, such love is natural to us who share the same Spirit. How can we not love those whom God and Christ love? You cannot love Christ and hate his bride. You must love what he loves. You must love believers, even those who can be very unlovable. God's love led to action. God's love led to sacrifice. Our love must be no different.

Speaking to his disciples, Christ highlights the importance of a loving attitude toward one another: "A new commandment I give to you, that you love one another: just as I have loved you, you also are to love one another. By this all people will know that you are my disciples, if you have love for one another" (John 13:34–35).

Why is this old commandment called "new"? Surely this injunction is a paraphrase of several Old Testament laws, is it not? Christ's words to his disciples in John 13:34–35 remind us of the commands in Deuteronomy 15:12–18 and Leviticus 19:33–34 ("you shall love him as yourself").

The command in the Old Testament to love "as I have loved you" refers specifically to the exodus of God's people out of Egypt. God's gracious dealings with his "treasured possession" (the indicative) provide the reason why they in turn should show the same type of graciousness (the imperative).

In comparison, Christ's words "as I have loved you" (John 13:34) are directly connected to his act of humiliation in John 13 (foot washing) and his sacrificial death on the cross (Phil. 2:5–11). Christ's humiliation and sacrifice point to a new way in which believers are to love one another. If our love never reaches to the place of sacrifice, then we have not loved as God desires us to love. His love involves sacrifice. Husbands, therefore, show their love for their wives in sacrificial love (Eph. 5:25).

Galatians 5:14 speaks of fulfilling "the whole law" when you love your neighbor as yourself. But while Paul applies the law generally in Galatians 5:14, he is also not afraid to apply the law specifically, in its Decalogue form, in other passages, such as Romans 13:8–10 and Ephesians 6:2–3.

If you have trouble loving others, think of the burden that God bore to show his love for you. If that cannot cure us of our self-love and dislike of others, especially regarding our brothers and sisters in Christ, I'm afraid nothing else will adequately remedy our problem. Also, remember that God commands us to love because, when we are like him, we find joy in loving, even when it is painful. Keep in mind that God's love is a blessed love that brings him satisfaction. Christ's love for us was a painful love that brought him satisfaction. And our love for God, which is shown in our love for others, will bring us both satisfaction and blessedness.

17

GOD IS GOOD

Give thanks to the LORD, for he is good,
for his steadfast love endures forever.

Psalm 136:1

Doctrine

God is good and necessarily so. God's essence does not conform to some external standard of goodness. God is essentially goodness itself. This essential attribute of God means that his other attributes (e.g., power, wisdom) are aspects of his goodness. His essence is good, so that he cannot do anything that is not good. Perfect goodness belongs to God alone: "And Jesus said to him, 'Why do you call me good? No one is good except God alone'" (Mark 10:18). Anything truly good in a creature simply mirrors God's goodness. Among his ethical attributes, Bavinck maintains, "first place is due to God's goodness."[1]

God communicates his goodness according to his will, what theologians have called his *outward works*. We come to understand his goodness as he manifests it among his creatures according to his will of decree. Thus, his goodness extends to all creatures. Creation and providence are effects of his goodness. Yet those whom God has created and preserves according to his wisdom, power, and goodness are not necessarily objects of his mercy in Christ Jesus—though there is a type of mercy shown to the nonelect in not giving them in this life what they deserve. Thus, his goodness exhibits a wider scope than his mercy. If man had not sinned, the Son would have become incarnate—if at all—as an act of God's goodness, not of his mercy, because humans would not have been considered fallen creatures.

God created everything good, and such goodness can be received from God alone, the fountain and spring of all goodness. Importantly, God possesses goodness not as a quality but of his very nature, "not a habit added to his essence, but his essence itself," as Charnock attests; "he is not first God, and then afterwards good; but he is good as he is God, his essence, being one and the same, is formally and equally God and good."[2]

God's goodness, like his other attributes, is infinite, yet he freely extends it to his creatures. Those who receive benefits because of the goodness of God can be good themselves, which shows that this attribute, unlike infinity, eternality, or immutability, is, analogically speaking, communicable. Thus, God loves not only his own goodness but also that which he communicates to his creatures. As Charnock says, "If he loves himself, he cannot but love the resemblance of himself, and the image of his own goodness."[3] In creating, then, he necessarily loves his creation, because in its essential (yet derived) goodness, creation resembles himself.

Still, God's goodness allows him to relate to his creation freely, not coercively, in a good and bountiful manner, which is most pleasing to him. That is, his decision to create was free, but in his creative activity, he necessarily made everything good: "And God saw everything that he had made, and behold, it was very good. And there was evening and there was morning, the sixth day" (Gen. 1:31). In summary, anything God creates must be good.

In the words of Charnock, "As it is the perfection of his nature, it is necessary; as it is the communication of his bounty, it is voluntary."[4] The motive for creating must come from within God, not from without. Wisdom speaks to God's work of directing and accomplishing creation, but goodness provides the motive. In fact, God could have no end but himself as the supreme good. Thus, God by necessity wills the good as an end, but the means that lead to the end he wills freely.

Regarding Adam's state in the garden of Eden, God displayed his goodness to Adam by offering him a gracious reward for his obedience. Adam owed God obedience, Charnock observes, but "the article on God's part, of giving perpetual blessedness to innocent man, was not founded upon rules of strict justice and righteousness, for that would have argued God to be a debtor to man."[5] The reward offered by God—whether immortality or eternal life—far exceeded what Adam could merit, which testifies to God's goodness in creation. Similarly, goodness was also the "spring of redemption," manifested as "pure goodness," for God was not required to redeem fallen humanity.[6]

God's goodness provides the reason why God redeemed men and women through his Son. This goodness exceeds that revealed in creation, for, Charnock maintains, "there is more of his bounty expressed in that one verse, 'God so loved the world, that he gave his only begotten Son' (John 3:16), than there is in the whole volume of the world: it is an incomprehensible *so*; a *so* that all the angels in heaven cannot analyze."[7]

God so loved a sinful, rebellious world at enmity with him. That's what makes his love so wondrous, namely, that he loves the unlovable and undeserving.

Goodness in and through Christ[8]

Christians affirm God's goodness, but just how good is he? We can speak of him being "infinitely good," but that still doesn't help the person in the pew much. People need specifics. Is it possible that God could show more goodness to his people than to his beloved Son?

Think of the truth that the Father poured out wrath on his Son in whom he has been eternally well pleased (Matt. 3:17; 17:5).

How do we understand this mystery? In one sense, we can say that God was never happier with his Son than when he was most angry with him. What does that mean? As John Owen explains,

> [The Father] was always well pleased with the holiness of [Christ's] person, the excellency and perfections of his righteousness, and the sweetness of his obedience, but he was displeased with the sins that were charged on him: and therefore it pleased him to bruise him and put him to grief with whom he was always well pleased.[9]

This understanding of our redemption leads us to say something rather provocative: that the goodness shown to us, God's people, is "a greater goodness to us, than was for a time manifested to Christ himself."[10]

God's wrath on his Son was so intense that it could have sunk millions of worlds of sinful men and angels. The Father forsook his Son for a moment in order that the Father would never forsake us (Heb. 13:5), a promise Christ never received. The Holy One of God was declared at Calvary to be unholy, so that unholy creatures like us might be declared holy as he is holy. God valued the redemption of the elect so much that he sentenced his own Son to humiliation on earth so that all who belong to Christ might be exalted in heaven. Thus, in speaking about the goodness of God, we must speak vividly, sometimes provocatively, about the way in which his goodness is shown to us. Charnock models such speech well:

> God was desirous to hear him groaning, and see him bleeding, that we might not groan under his frowns, and bleed under his wrath; he spared not him, that he might spare us; refused not to strike him, that he might be well pleased with us; drenched his sword in the blood of his Son, that it might not for ever be wet with ours, but that his goodness might for ever triumph in our salvation; he was willing to have his Son made man, and die, rather than man should perish, who had delighted to ruin himself; he seemed to degrade him for a time from what he was.[11]

To affirm that for a time God showed more goodness to us than to his Son is to say that Christ's shrieks, cries, and spiritual agonies were not pretended but real. Can we conceive of a higher love than that which brings God to show more love to us than his beloved Son? It is impossible to conceive of a more shocking but beautiful display of his love for us.

We are living in an age, I believe, where preaching has fallen on hard times. There are many reasons for this, but one reason is that pastors have a limited vocabulary and ability to express God's attributes to his people. As a result, they do not paint vivid pictures of God's goodness, love, patience, wrath, and so forth, in order to move congregants to respond to these glorious truths. God is good. Fine! But how is God good? The preacher must creatively and convincingly unfold these perfections so Christians can understand, love, and believe God's goodness to them.

The highest gift possible for the Father to bestow on his people was that of his Son, the one to whom he showed, for a period, less goodness than he showed to vile, God-hating sinners like you and me. As we reflect on such an expression of God's goodness, we must also be moved by the fact that the one who for no reason merited divine wrath, received what we deserved. Amazingly, for a time, Christ received more wrath and we more love.

Application

God is good, and for that reason, we must love him for this attribute and must participate in this goodness by "tasting" and "seeing" that the Lord is good (Ps. 34:8). This we should do especially in the sacrament of the Lord's Supper. The Lord's Supper presents God's people with a wonderful context for pausing and meditating on the gospel. In life we all hurry about, often acting alone in a busy world. But in the Lord's Supper we are forced, in a manner of speaking, to sit, think, and taste real goodness—for there we taste the Lord Jesus.

As we recognize God's goodness to us in Christ, we should

desire to learn his ways and commands for our lives, because we trust that his ways are good ways: "You are good and do good; teach me your statutes" (Ps. 119:68). As children of our heavenly Father belonging to Christ and indwelt by the Spirit, we make it our aim to do good. In light of what God has done for us, we must "not grow weary of doing good, for in due season we will reap, if we do not give up. So then, as we have opportunity, let us do good to everyone, and especially to those who are of the household of faith" (Gal. 6:9–10). Christ himself went about doing good (Acts 10:38) even in the greatest suffering, leaving us a pattern and example (1 Pet. 2:20–21).

If we cannot do good, serious questions have to be asked whether we have really understood God's goodness to us in Christ. Grasping this truth alone should sufficiently motivate us to shower others with good deeds. In fact, our gospel witness is built on both our message and our deeds. Writing to Titus, Paul implores him, "Show yourself in all respects to be a model of good works" (Titus 2:7). Of course, such works have been prepared in advance for us to do (Eph. 2:10), but that does not stop the biblical authors from commanding believers to do them. Likewise, we need to understand what constitutes such works, and the Westminster Confession of Faith provides an instructive summary: "Good works are only such as God hath commanded in his holy Word, and not such as, without the warrant thereof, are devised by men, out of blind zeal, or upon any pretense of good intention" (16.1). Our good God alone gets to define a "good" work, and he does so in his Word.

Out of his goodness, God delights to accept our good works. In the sixteenth century, Benedict Pictet wrote,

> These good works are performed by the faithful, and although they are not perfect, yet they may truly be called good, because they are wrought by the special motion of the Holy Spirit living in their hearts, and by the assistance of God's grace from which they please God and from which God promises to them themselves a reward.[12]

God's goodness is highlighted by the fact that he not only accepts our imperfect works in Christ as good but also rewards them because he has determined that they are good. Again, the Westminster Confession helps us: "The persons of believers being accepted through Christ, their good works also are accepted in him" (16.6). Thus, we affirm that God accepts us because of the perfect righteousness of Christ, which is ours by imputation. Likewise, our imperfect works also find their acceptance in our Savior. But alongside these truths, God shows his goodness in rewarding us for our good works that are truly performed and accomplished in Christ. Besides the giving of his Son, God shows his goodness toward us in every way possible for a Father toward his children.

18

GOD IS PATIENT

But you, O Lord, are a God merciful and gracious,
slow to anger and abounding in steadfast love
and faithfulness.

Psalm 86:15

Doctrine

God's patience is, as far as sinners are concerned, a highly treasured attribute among his people: "But you are a God ready to
forgive, gracious and merciful, slow to anger and abounding in
steadfast love, and did not forsake them" (Neh. 9:17). But the
patience of God does not today receive the emphasis it should,
especially in preaching. In his mercy, God has a certain disposition
toward sinful creatures, but his patience has in view the delaying
or tempering of the punishment that sinners deserve.

Edward Leigh understands the patience of God as that attribute "whereby he bears the reproach of sinners and defers their
punishments; or it is the most bountiful will of God, whereby
he does long bear with sin which he hates, sparing sinners, not
minding their destruction, but that he might bring them to repentance."[1] This view, then, presents a twofold understanding of
God's patience, either deferred punishment in itself or deferred
punishment issuing forth in redemption.

Divine patience must not be understood as God suffering (i.e., being passible). This does not contradict what I said earlier about being able to affirm in a sense that "God died (suffered) on the cross." This statement holds true in a sense only in reference to the concrete person of Christ (in the union of his divine and human natures) and not to God in an abstract or general manner, as we are discussing here. In brief, Reformed theologians have generally understood God's patience as that attribute whereby he delays the execution of his judgment in its fullest extent.

Charnock elaborates: "[Patience] signifies a willingness to defer, and an unwillingness to pour forth wrath upon sinful creatures; [God] moderates his provoked justice, and forbears to revenge the injuries he daily meets with in the world."[2] Charnock deftly brings God's attributes together harmoniously as the logical outcome of his essential simplicity: "Goodness sets God upon the exercise of patience, and patience sets many a sinner on running into the arms of mercy."[3]

Having said that, God's patience does not extend to fallen angels. Though they are spared their ultimate punishment for a time, they do not have an opportunity to repent and be forgiven. God does not show mercy to them in the sense that he does to fallen sinners. Thus, mercy and patience are necessarily and closely tied together in God's dealings with sinful humanity.

God's patience does not make him weak, and his slowness to anger (Ex. 34:6; Ps. 103:8) does not make him incapable of anger. When promises are delayed, there resides no slackness in God. Likewise, we must not view God as a pushover just because he temporarily withholds punishments. God has complete knowledge of the thoughts and actions of all creatures all at once in his eternally present eye. Just because he does not now exercise power to punish does not imply that he lacks such power to do so. Instead, his complete power and exhaustive knowledge explain why God can exercise such patience:

> The LORD is slow to anger and great in power,
> and the LORD will by no means clear the guilty.
> His way is in whirlwind and storm,
> and the clouds are the dust of his feet. (Nah. 1:3)

God does not need to be in a rush. His patience is his power, and when he exercises the former, he shows more of the latter than he would if he created a thousand worlds. How? Creating worlds shows a power over creatures and matter; exercising patience shows power over himself. We often think of God's patience in relation to his goodness and mercy, and rightly so: "The LORD, the LORD, a God merciful and gracious, slow to anger, and abounding in steadfast love and faithfulness" (Ex. 34:6; see also Ps. 86:15). But his power, knowledge, and eternity, for example, are also vital components of divine patience.

Christ's Death Reveals God's Patience

Fundamental to the understanding of divine patience is the death of Christ. We can only explain God's patience toward human beings and not toward angels in light of Christ's sacrificial atonement. He took the nature of humans ("the seed of Abraham") and not of angels so that humanity should benefit from God's patience.

God's patience toward humankind arises out of the gospel and the covenant of grace. Without Christ's appointment as Mediator, God has no reason to be patient toward sinners. He may be good toward his creatures apart from Christ—though some would dispute that—but God cannot be merciful or patient toward sinful humanity apart from the person and work of his Son.

According to Charnock, God destroys the ungodly with "some regret," and he delivers his judgments by degrees. He "pinches" rather than tearing asunder.[4] In all God does, he exercises equity, but in what we deserve, there is no equality. In other words, all receive better than what they deserve while on this earth. Even the wicked prosper for a time. Edward Leigh quotes

Samuel Bolton as saying, "If but any tender-hearted man should sit one hour in the Throne of the Almighty, and look down upon the earth as God does continually, and see what abominations are done in that hour, he would undoubtedly in the next set all the world on fire."[5]

The wickedness of man remains an affront to God, but he nevertheless exercises patience by delaying and tempering his wrath. His punishments in this world, as horrible as some of them may be, are still disproportionate to the demerit of sin against an infinitely holy and righteous God.

But why does God temper his judgments and show such patience? The answer given above has in view the mediatorial work of Christ. This is certainly the main reason, but the patience of God toward sinners on account of Christ also shows God to be appeasable. God desires reconciliation with his creatures, and so he does not destroy them at once but gives them space for repentance:

> But do not overlook this one fact, beloved, that with the Lord one day is as a thousand years, and a thousand years as one day. The Lord is not slow to fulfill his promise as some count slowness, but is patient toward you, not wishing that any should perish, but that all should reach repentance. (2 Pet. 3:8–9)

Notice that God's desire to be reconciled relates not only to his patience but also to his eternality ("one day is as a thousand years").

Practically speaking, the patience of God also allows for the propagation of the human race. Mankind could not increase in number if God killed all humans on their entry into the world (or on their conception). More specifically, his patience allows for the continuance and growth of the church. God has in his eye the elect who sometimes spring from the loins of evil men, as righteous Hezekiah was born of his wicked father, Ahaz. In this light, Charnock observes, "There could not have been a saint in the earth, nor, consequently, in heaven, had it not been for this perfection"—that is, his patience.[6]

This explains, then, why God is patient, even toward wicked men. And for those who are not brought to repentance by his patience, he will surely execute his justice on them. All this suggests that his patience is either directly or indirectly focused on Christ. In and through Christ, and for his sake, God continues to exercise patience toward his creatures.

Application

God is patient with us because he does not need to worry about us. He knows, without any hint of anxiety, how all things will work out. When we as finite creatures are impatient, however, we sometimes show anxiety or frustration about the outcome.

God knows the outcome of our sanctification not only in this life but also in the life to come. He may allow us to take one step backward for the moment if he knows we will take two steps forward in the future. This never justifies our sin, but it does manifest his forbearance toward us while sin remains. Hence, his patience toward us never comes as something bare but rather as that accompanied by his wisdom and love. Here we return, as we must again and again, to his divine simplicity. He does nothing to us that does not involve all of who he is.

We can look back on events in our lives when God could have justly cast us into outer darkness but did not. Even our sins he can use for his glory (Gen. 50:20). When we consider the glories of God's wise and loving patience toward us in Christ Jesus, then we are better prepared to display patience toward others as we seek to imitate God's patience and see the Spirit's fruit in our lives. Charnock rightly says, "He is unlike God, that is hurried with an unruly impetus to punish others for wronging him."[7] And he adds,

> God has exercised a long-suffering from the fall of Adam to this minute on innumerable subjects, and shall we be transported with a desire of revenge upon a single injury? . . . How distant are they

from the nature of God, who are in a flame upon every slight provocation, from a sense of some feeble and imaginary honour, that must bloody their sword for a trifle, and write their revenge in wounds and death.[8]

As is so often the case, our attitude toward others must be governed by God's patient attitude toward us.

19

GOD IS MERCIFUL

For the LORD your God is a merciful God. He will
not leave you or destroy you or forget the covenant
with your fathers that he swore to them.

Deuteronomy 4:31

Doctrine

God is merciful, a truth that Christians, when falling on their knees
in prayer, often confess first from their lips: "God, be merciful to
me, a sinner!" (Luke 18:13). As sinners, we count this attribute as
exceedingly precious, and God does as well. Mercy is properly an
affection related to the divine will, whereby God has compassion on
fallen creatures. As Thomas Goodwin puts it so beautifully, "Says
God, All that you know by me is, that I will save poor sinners, that I
delight in mercy. I care not who knows this."[1] Thus, when we speak
of mercy, we tend to refer to God's lovingkindness, forbearance, or
pity toward those with no claim to it as wretched sinners.

The speaker in Lamentations 3 understands this attribute well:

The steadfast love of the LORD never ceases;
    his mercies never come to an end;
they are new every morning;
    great is your faithfulness.

God Is Merciful

"The LORD is my portion," says my soul,
     "therefore I will hope in him." (Lam. 3:22–24)

In the Scriptures, this affection is usually spoken of, as here, in relation to other affections and attributes, such as God's goodness and faithfulness.

Over the centuries, the attribute of God's mercy has been used to argue in an unorthodox manner that God feels the misery of others. In fact, his mercy does not mean that his heart becomes miserable, as if there is a passion in him that changes his being. Rather, God in mercy seeks to give relief to those who do not deserve it. Indeed, the proper notion of mercy may be understood as God first "taking our misery to heart" and then giving relief to the miserable.

God possesses infinite knowledge of himself, leading him to necessarily love and glorify himself. But he in no way needs to be merciful to himself. Out of his essential goodness and love, God shows mercy to unworthy objects: "Remember your mercy, O LORD, and your steadfast love, for they have been from of old. Remember not the sins of my youth or my transgressions; according to your steadfast love remember me, for the sake of your goodness, O LORD!" (Ps. 25:6–7).

God remains sovereign and free in his mercy, and he thus glories in his expression of it (Ex. 33:19). God, as essentially good and merciful, calls judgment his "alien" (i.e., strange) work (Isa. 28:21). In contrast, Thomas Watson calls mercy God's "darling attribute, which he most delights in."[2]

Willful, unrepentant sin causes God to send judgment, but he delights in his merciful love:

Who is a God like you, pardoning iniquity
     and passing over transgression
     for the remnant of his inheritance?
He does not retain his anger forever,
     because he delights in steadfast love. (Mic. 7:18)

150

When God shows mercy, he reveals his glory. So, for example, God "stood" with Moses on Mount Sinai (Ex. 34:5), and his message to Moses highlighted his merciful character:

> The LORD passed before him and proclaimed, "The LORD, the LORD, a God merciful and gracious, slow to anger, and abounding in steadfast love and faithfulness, keeping steadfast love for thousands, forgiving iniquity and transgression and sin, but who will by no means clear the guilty, visiting the iniquity of the fathers on the children and the children's children, to the third and the fourth generation." (Ex. 34:6–7)

Scripture sometimes contrasts God's mercy with man's: "Then David said to Gad, 'I am in great distress. Let us fall into the hand of the LORD, for his mercy is great; but let me not fall into the hand of man'" (2 Sam. 24:14). God's mercy is the basis for the mercy we show to others in their misery: "Blessed be the God and Father of our Lord Jesus Christ, the Father of mercies and God of all comfort, who comforts us in all our affliction, so that we may be able to comfort those who are in any affliction, with the comfort with which we ourselves are comforted by God" (2 Cor. 1:3–4). If we compare our mercy with God's, we can rightly call ours a form of cruelty, so infinitely distant is ours from God's.

God's mercy should also be understood under the two categories of *general* and *special* mercy. So Francis Turretin argues,

> To be able to know God as merciful by a general mercy tending to some temporal good and the delay of punishment is far different from being able to know him as merciful by a mercy special and saving in Christ after a satisfaction has been made. To be able to know him as placable and benign is different from being able to know him as actually appeased or certainly to be appeased. We grant that the heathen could have the former from the light of nature, but not the latter which nevertheless is necessarily required to tranquilize the conscience.[3]

God feeds the hungry (Ps. 104:27); he gives air for all to breath; he provides the means for us to make medicine for relieving the sick. God shows general mercy to all his creatures. To some, even those outside the covenant of grace, God shows varying degrees of mercy, because, as God, he has no obligation to man. But his special mercy results from the person and work of his Son on behalf of the church.

God's Merciful Provision in Christ

If we are to have any hope as miserable sinners, we must seek the special mercy that comes through Christ and rejoice in it once we find it:

> Blessed be the God and Father of our Lord Jesus Christ! According to his great mercy, he has caused us to be born again to a living hope through the resurrection of Jesus Christ from the dead, to an inheritance that is imperishable, undefiled, and unfading, kept in heaven for you, who by God's power are being guarded through faith for a salvation ready to be revealed in the last time. (1 Pet. 1:3–5)

God gives us hope, grants us an inheritance, and guards us by his power—none of which we deserve. Why? Because of his "great mercy." What makes his mercy so great? That his great Son died for our sins and was raised from the dead in order that we might be "born again to a living hope."

The free, eternal, and overflowing mercy of God toward us sweetens our affections for God. Thomas Brooks delights in such mercy:

> It is free mercy that every day keeps hell and my soul asunder; it is mercy that daily pardons my sins; it is mercy that supplies all my inward and outward wants; it is mercy that preserves, and feeds, and clothes my outward man; and it is mercy that renews, strengthens, and prospers my inward man; it is mercy that has kept me many times from committing such and such sins; it is

mercy that has kept me many a time from falling before such and such temptations; it is mercy that has many a time preserved me from being swallowed up by such and such inward and outward afflictions.[4]

Because God has shown mercy to us specifically in Christ, he will bestow on us all mercies. He is the Father of mercies to us (2 Cor. 1:3), and every good and perfect gift that we receive comes from our merciful heavenly Father (James 1:17). We receive these mercies because Christ's death and resurrection have great power for us in their working—so much that nothing can separate us from God's love. Thus, God desires, for the sake of Christ, to shower us in mercies, so that Christ may have his proper inheritance. Thomas Goodwin rightly concludes that God's mercy and grace are "his greatest riches and highest glory"; they are "the richest jewels in his crown."[5]

God reveals his heart to us in the heart of Christ. According to John Owen, "Mercy in God is but a naked simple apprehension of misery, made effective by an act of his holy will to relieve. Mercy in Christ is a compassion, a condolency, and has a moving of pity and sorrow joined with it."[6] This is an important distinction between the mercy of God and the mercy of Christ.

Many New Testament books offer us wonderful glimpses into the human nature of Christ, yet Hebrews perhaps stands out in this respect. The main thrust of Hebrews 1 is to show Christ's superiority to the angels because he is the divine Son (vv. 8–12). But in chapter 2, Christ's humanity comes into focus. Christ shares in our "flesh and blood" (v. 14), and he is made "like his brothers in every respect" so that he can be our merciful High Priest (v. 17). Christ could of course be merciful since God is merciful, but without sharing in our humanity, Christ could not be a merciful High Priest.

A high priest must be able to sympathize with the people he represents. As our High Priest, Christ experienced miseries, sufferings, and temptations on earth, which were possible because he had assumed a human nature in a world full of sin and misery. In the words of John Owen, Christ "had particular experience thereby of the weakness, sorrows, and miseries of human nature under the assaults of temptations; he tried it, felt it, and will never forget it."[7] In this light, Christ will relieve, favor, and comfort his people by his grace. His experiences on earth did not "add" to his mercifulness, but they did make him more ready to dispense grace to those who require it. Owen claims that Christ "bears still in his holy mind the sense he had of his sorrows wherewith he was pressed in the time of his temptations, and thereon seeing his brethren conflicting with the like difficulties is ready to help them."[8] Owen is arguing that Christ's human experiences on earth, in a manner of speaking, were as beneficial for him as they are for us. What a wonderful mystery.

In the end, the incarnation opens up a way for God to be merciful that would otherwise be impossible. God remains so intent on showing mercy that he sends his Son into the world—one full of sin and misery—to take on flesh so that he can show sympathy to us based on his own human experience.

Application

The emotion we find most frequently attributed to Jesus during the course of his earthly ministry is mercy. Christ, anointed with the Spirit, "went about doing good and healing all who were oppressed by the devil, for God was with him" (Acts 10:38).

Jesus was often "moved with pity" toward others (Mark 1:41; see also Matt. 9:36; 14:14; 20:34). But Christ extended mercy not simply toward people in their physical or spiritual suffering (e.g., demon possession); he showed pity toward the whole person (Mark 6:34). He sought ways to be merciful.

Very often in the Christian life, we are too reactionary, always having to respond to situations and then not as we should. One way for us to respond better comes through understanding our holy Savior's mercy to us and pursuing Christian holiness. These actions will lead us to show mercy to others and to relieve others of their physical and spiritual misery while treating them as whole people.

The Christian who has received mercy seeks to show it. Knowing includes experiencing. Indeed, Christ issues a rather startling command in his Sermon on the Mount concerning the need for us to show mercy: "Blessed are the merciful, for they shall receive mercy" (Matt. 5:7).

Thomas Watson quotes the early church father Ambrose as saying, "The sum and definition of religion is, Be rich in works of mercy, be helpful to the bodies and souls of others. Scatter your golden seeds; let the lamp of your profession be filled with the oil of charity. Be merciful in giving and forgiving."[9] Here Ambrose understands our duty to the whole person: body and soul. God's mercy and our mercy are not mere concepts or ideas but actions toward others.

In expressing spiritual mercy, we must show mercy to those who have sinned against us. Like our Father in heaven, we should be more willing to show mercy than the offender was willing to sin against us. Thomas Watson observes,

> Thus Stephen the proto-martyr, "He kneeled down and cried with a loud voice, Lord, lay not this sin to their charge" (Acts 7:60). When he prayed for himself he stood—but when he came to pray for his enemies, he kneeled down, to show, says Bernard, his earnestness in prayer and how greatly he desired that God would forgive them. This is a rare kind of mercy. "It is a man's glory to pass over a transgression" (Proverbs 19:11). Mercy in forgiving injuries, as it is the touchstone, so the crown of Christianity. Cranmer was of a merciful disposition. If any who had wronged him came to ask a favor from him, he would do all that lay in his power for him, insomuch that it grew to a proverb: "Do Cranmer an injury and he will be your friend as long as he lives." To "overcome evil with good," and answer malice with mercy is truly heroic, and renders piety glorious in the eyes of all.[10]

In sum, "Be merciful, even as your Father is merciful" (Luke 6:36).

20

GOD IS WISE

Where is the one who is wise? Where is the scribe? Where is the debater of this age? Has not God made foolish the wisdom of the world? For since, in the wisdom of God, the world did not know God through wisdom, it pleased God through the folly of what we preach to save those who believe. For Jews demand signs and Greeks seek wisdom, but we preach Christ crucified, a stumbling block to Jews and folly to Gentiles, but to those who are called, both Jews and Greeks, Christ the power of God and the wisdom of God. For the foolishness of God is wiser than men, and the weakness of God is stronger than men.

1 Corinthians 1:20–25

Doctrine

Some might place God's wisdom in the context of his knowledge and understanding—that is, his omniscience—but wisdom deserves its own separate treatment as an essential attribute of God. He is "wise in heart and mighty in strength" (Job 9:4). Paul calls him the "only wise God" (Rom. 16:27). He is perfectly, universally, perpetually, incomprehensibly, and infallibly wise. Of course, his wisdom must be consistent with his other attributes, yet this is simply another reason why he alone is properly wise.

Divine wisdom has in view God's ability (i.e., power) to act for a right end. The end reveals not only his wisdom but also the means that lead to that end. By his knowledge God discerns things, and by his wisdom, he acts on such understanding. Knowledge concerns the theoretical and wisdom the practical. Edward Leigh states,

> God's knowledge differs from his wisdom in our apprehension thus: his knowledge is conceived as the mere apprehension of every object, but his wisdom is conceived as that whereby he does order and dispose all things. His knowledge is conceived as an act; his wisdom as an habit or inward principle; not that it is so, but only we apprehend it in this manner.[1]

God in wisdom skillfully manages all things, ordering them according to his infinite understanding. He has no counselor (Rom. 11:34), for he possesses an essential and comprehensive wisdom (Job 12:13). And he displays his wisdom in the creation and government of all things:

> It is he who made the earth by his power,
>> who established the world by his wisdom,
>> and by his understanding stretched out the heavens.
> When he utters his voice, there is a tumult of waters in the
>> heavens,
>> and he makes the mist rise from the ends of the earth.
> He makes lightning for the rain,
>> and he brings forth the wind from his storehouses.
>> (Jer. 10:12–13)

> O LORD, how manifold are your works!
>> In wisdom have you made them all;
>> the earth is full of your creatures. (Ps. 104:24)

The creation of the universe remains a monument of God's

powerful wisdom. He orders all things in their place: "You have fixed all the boundaries of the earth; you have made summer and winter" (Ps. 74:17). According to Calvin, the creation of human bodies "shows itself to be a composition so ingenious that its Artificer is rightly judged a wonder-worker."[2]

God displays his wisdom not only in creation but also in his works of providence, whereby he guides and directs all things to their proper end. To see God's wise providence at play, one has only to read the moving story of Joseph and to observe the divine wisdom stamped all over the various events that led to the fulfillment of his original dream (Gen. 37:5–8; 50:18–20). God's ways are wise ways; his wisdom, being infinite, should cause us, at times, to be perplexed at what he does providentially in our lives. Mary could probably not have conceived anything worse than seeing her son crucified before her very eyes, but God could not have planned anything better.

Christ as the Wisdom of God[3]

The Son of God exists as the personal wisdom of God. Christ manifests wisdom as a necessary perfection of God. God's secrets, mysteries, and purposes were all darkly veiled until the Son of God appeared and opened up the wisdom of the Father to us. Owen believes that we can only behold the infinite, manifold wisdom of God in the person of the Son: "It is in Christ alone that we can discern anything of it; for him has the Father chosen and sealed to represent it unto us. All the treasures of this wisdom are hid, laid up, and laid out in him."[4]

Christ received the necessary gifts and graces to be able to perform his duty as a prophet. Besides his natural abilities, Christ also had a "peculiar endowment of the Spirit, without and beyond the bounds of all comprehensible measures, that he was to receive as the great prophet of the church, in whom the Father would speak and give out the last revelation of himself."[5] Thus, Owen writes, "All the mysteries of the counsel between the Father and the eternal

Word for the salvation of the elect, with all the way whereby it was to be accomplished, through his own blood, were known unto him."[6] Unlike Moses, who was given revelations at particular times, Christ possessed all the treasures of wisdom, knowledge, and truth. More than any other prophet before him, he could speak infallibly and with authority about the mind of God.

As noted, God manifests his wisdom in the creation and government of his creatures, but his wisdom in redemption "mounts the mind to a greater astonishment."[7] In his typically splendid way of capturing the glories of salvation, Charnock refers to creation as the "footsteps" of God's wisdom and to the work of redemption as the "face" of that wisdom.[8]

In redemption, multiple ends and means display the glory of God in his wisdom. For example, in the gospel one learns of the blessed union of the two natures in one person, the Lord Jesus Christ. The Christian life also displays how the first will be last and the last will be first (Matt. 20:16). And God's people learn that the way to glory is through shame and suffering, as it was for Christ himself.

Christ's work manifests the wisdom of God as he is both just and the justifier of the ungodly, but his person also reveals God's preeminent wisdom. For in the incarnation the finite unites with the infinite, immortality with mortality, and the one who ordains the law lives under it.

In short, the incarnation reveals the wisdom of God in appointing the Son as Mediator. Only the God-man could effect reconciliation between God and man, and communion with God remains possible for us only because God became man. Indeed, the incarnation of the second person of the Trinity gave him, according to his human nature, an experiential compassion that the divine nature could not offer. So the efficacy of Christ's priestly office, in all its aspects, depends on the union of the two natures in one person. The incarnation, then, is one of the many ways in which God has revealed his wisdom to men.

Thomas Ridgley correctly claims that the wisdom of God "appears yet more eminently in the work of our redemption. This work is what 'the angels desire to look into,' and cannot behold without the greatest admiration; for herein God's 'manifold wisdom' is displayed."[9]

Application

Very often we find ourselves as Christians wondering why God does something in our lives. We cannot fathom his purposes. But if we affirm his infinite wisdom, then we can humble ourselves in the midst of his providential workings in our circumstances. We lack his wisdom to make perfect sense of all that he does. Knowing that he possesses such wisdom allows us to trust him and entrust our situation, even in the direst circumstances, to him.

This trust should not, however, keep us from asking God for more wisdom. Solomon asked God for wisdom (1 Kings 3:9). And James says, "If any of you lacks wisdom, let him ask God, who gives generously to all without reproach, and it will be given him" (James 1:5). As God's creatures made in his image, we can become wise, even if only derivatively so. In God resides the fountain of wisdom, and he bestows on us this gift through Christ.

We are to have the mind of Christ (1 Cor. 2:16), especially insofar as we seek to understand and do God's will in a way that brings him glory and reveals our constant attitude of worship. Only with a Christian mind, whereby the Spirit leads us, are we able to understand the wisdom of God. By following the Spirit's guidance, we can comprehend our suffering in light of Christ's and our future glory in light of his. We love service because Christ became a servant, and we love our enemies because Christ loved his. In other words, to apply knowledge wisely simply means to apply the mind of Christ to every situation. Only then can we, in the midst of trials and persecutions, count it all joy (Rom. 8:18; James 1:2).

21

GOD IS HOLY

Who is like you, O Lord, among the gods?
Who is like you, majestic in holiness,
awesome in glorious deeds, doing wonders?
Exodus 15:11

Doctrine

Some have called God's holiness the center of his communicable attributes. This may not be the best expression since all of God's attributes are grounded on one another. As we have mentioned, God's holiness is his goodness is his power is his wisdom, and so forth. There really is no central attribute in God. Nonetheless, when he does anything in terms of his outward will, it is necessarily holy because of God's essential holiness. By implication, he remains just in all his works. Not surprisingly, this attribute has received a great deal of attention in the writings of Christian theologians over the centuries.

God's holiness has been described as the "beauty" of all his attributes, "without which," argues Leigh, "his wisdom would be but subtlety, his justice cruelty, his Sovereignty tyranny, his mercy foolish pity."[1] Far from being an infinite monster, observes Charnock, God possesses a "perfect and unpolluted freedom from all evil."[2] Charnock further describes God's holiness as the "rectitude or integrity of the Divine nature . . . in affection and action to the Divine will . . . , whereby he works with a becomingness to his own excellency."[3] Simply put, God unchangeably loves good and hates evil.

Reformed theologians unanimously agree that holiness is an essential attribute of God. As his attributes are woven together in our finite conception, we are able to paint a more accurate picture of him in his essence. When we conceive of him, we must remember that his holiness is as necessary an attribute as God's being, omniscience, and immutability. To speak properly, they are all as necessary as each other because the attributes cannot be divided.

In emphasizing this perfection, the Bible presents God as the "Holy One" (Job 6:10; Isa. 40:25). The angels call to one another, saying,

> Holy, holy, holy is the LORD of hosts;
> the whole earth is full of his glory! (Isa. 6:3)

Similarly in Revelation, the four living creatures never cease to sing praise to God, saying,

> Holy, holy, holy, is the Lord God Almighty,
>   who was and is and is to come! (Rev. 4:8)

God possesses holiness without limit. Thus, while we derive our holiness from him through Christ, his holiness originates in himself. According to Leigh, "God's holiness is that excellency of his nature, by which he gives himself unto himself, doing all for himself, and in all, and by all, and above all, aiming at his own pleasure and glory; or it is the absolute purity of his nature and his abhorring of evil (Ex. 34:30; Rev. 15:4)."[4]

Thomas Watson speaks of God as holy in four ways:

1. Intrinsically: he is holy in his nature.
2. Primarily: he is the pattern of holiness.

3. Efficiently: he is the cause of all holiness in others, including Christ's human nature.
4. Transcendently: he is far above the capacity of the angels and glorified saints to behold.[5]

God's holiness is his beauty. In one of the most memorable phrases in Charnock's work on God's attributes, he argues, "Power is his hand and arm, omniscience his eye, mercy his bowels, eternity his duration, his holiness his beauty."[6] Thus, his absolute and infinite holiness implies beauty in the same measure. Creatures cannot be essentially holy because of their innate mutability, but the immutable God can be, in keeping with his other attributes.

In his holiness, God must necessarily abhor sin, and Charnock declares that since God loves himself, "so must he necessarily hate every thing that is against himself."[7] Thus, God hates sin intensely, as Charnock attests in view of scriptural teaching: "He is impatient of beholding it; the very sight of it affects him with detestation (Hab. 1:13); he hates the first spark of it in the imagination (Zech. 8:17)."[8]

In fact, Charnock maintains, "Sin is the only primary object of his displeasure."[9] Man derives his nature from God, so it is not the nature of man that God hates but rather the corruption of man's nature. For God to approve of sin, he must first deny himself, an utter impossibility. Therefore, God will perpetually hate sin and express his displeasure against it, which provides the ground for the doctrine of eternal punishment.

Holiness Displayed in Christ[10]

By the merits of Jesus Christ, sinners escape the punishment for sin, but God had to punish Christ by way of the cross in order to reconcile sinners to himself. In consistency with his other attributes, God's holiness and abhorrence for sin demanded justice. Charnock uses vivid imagery to capture this all-important point of Christian theology:

> Not all the vials of judgments, that have, or shall be poured out upon the wicked world, nor the flaming furnace of a sinner's conscience, nor the irreversible sentence pronounced against the rebellious devils, nor the groans of the damned creatures, give such a demonstration of God's hatred of sin, as the wrath of God let loose upon his Son.[11]

Charnock explains that the Father

> would have the most excellent person, one next in order to himself, and equal to him in all the glorious perfections of his nature (Phil. ii. 6), die on a disgraceful cross, and be exposed to the flames of Divine wrath, rather than sin should live, and his holiness remain for ever disparaged by the violations of his law. . . . God seems to lay aside the bowels of a father, and put on the garb of an irreconcilable enemy.[12]

Has the holiness of God ever been more beautifully displayed than in the ugliness of Christ's death on the cross? As we read in Psalm 22:1–3, holiness demanded that the Father forsake his Son on the cross. In terms of God "crushing" his Son, "justice indeed gave the stroke, but holiness ordered it."[13] Why did God become man? To bleed to death for sinners that he might satisfy the justice of his divine holiness.

God manifests his holiness not just in Christ's death but also in his person. He is the image of God's holiness. The incarnation makes it possible for the elect not only to look on the holiness of God that is otherwise too dazzling for us to behold but also through him to become holy like God. In Christ, we have a walking picture of the law, a reflection of God's holy character. What does holiness look like in concrete terms of what we can pursue? It looks like Christ.

God's holiness (and any other attribute, for that matter) would be too much for sinful human beings to bear if God did not relate to us by way of the Mediator. No wonder, then, that it was Christ and not the Father whom Isaiah saw in Isaiah 6: "Isaiah said these things because he saw his glory and spoke of him" (John 12:41).

The necessity that God reveals his holiness in and through Christ seems to be constantly overlooked in books on holiness. But a cursory glance at John Owen's treatise on the Holy Spirit shows just how important this concept is for our theology of holiness. In Owen's opinion, because we still have indwelling sin, the essential holiness of God (i.e., his infinite, eternal holiness) is not the "immediate ground and motive unto holiness; but it is the holiness of God as manifested and revealed unto us in Christ Jesus."[14]

We need an encouragement to holiness, which can only come through Jesus Christ based on what he has done for us and on how he has revealed God to us. Moreover, we cannot answer appropriately to God's holiness unless he condescends to us through his covenant, and he does so in the person of Christ.

All our current knowledge of God and his attributes, "unless it be that which we have in and by Jesus Christ, is insufficient to lead or conduct us in that life of faith and obedience which is necessary unto us."[15] As Christians, "with unveiled face" we behold the glory of Christ and are thus "transformed into the same image from one degree of glory to another" (2 Cor. 3:18). Paul carries on this point:

> For what we proclaim is not ourselves, but Jesus Christ as Lord, with ourselves as your servants for Jesus' sake. For God, who said, "Let light shine out of darkness," has shone in our hearts to give the light of the knowledge of the glory of God in the face of Jesus Christ. (2 Cor. 4:5–6)

The glory of God, which necessarily includes his holiness, is revealed to us in "the face of Jesus Christ."

Application

Holiness is not optional for the Christian: "Strive for peace with everyone, and for the holiness without which no one will see the

Lord" (Heb. 12:14). The holiness of God lies utterly beyond us as those who live with indwelling sin. Apart from Christ, God's essential holiness would destroy us, for he is "of purer eyes than to see evil" (Hab. 1:13). But in Christ, we can love and adore his holiness. We can also love the living image of his holiness in the person of Christ.

Our motivation and ability to be holy arises out of our great salvation through Christ, the Holy One of God, to whom we have been united by faith. The "Spirit of holiness" works such faith in us and sanctifies us in the very holiness of Christ of which we now have access (Rom. 1:4; 1 Cor. 1:30; 2 Thess. 2:13; Titus 3:5). In the process, we will be renewed in the image of Christ in "true righteousness and holiness" as we become more like him who saved us for himself (Eph. 4:24). Indeed, as we come to love Christ not only for what he has done but also for who he is, we will desire to be more and more like him in our thoughts, words, and deeds. However, holiness divorced from the gospel of Christ results in nothing more than legalistic externalism. We must beware of the subtle tendency to focus on Christian duty apart from the person of Christ, for such a soul-damning burden we cannot bear (Matt. 11:28).

Moreover, if we belong to Christ, we will suffer with him (Phil. 3:10; 1 Thess. 2:14–15). So in our quest for holiness, we do well to hear Paul's call to emulate the humble suffering of Christ: "Have this mind among yourselves, which is yours in Christ Jesus" (Phil. 2:5; see also 2:6–11). If we are in Christ, we must walk as he did (1 John 2:6). In fact, Romans 15 gives wonderful instruction on the practical implications of imitating Christ. In the gospel, Jesus provides the supreme pattern and example of holiness for us. Our goal in holiness must be to have the mind of Christ (1 Cor. 2:16).

Herman Bavinck makes an important point with regard to our holiness:

> To understand the benefit of sanctification correctly, we must proceed from the idea that Christ is our holiness in the same sense in

which he is our righteousness. He is a complete and all-sufficient Savior. He does not accomplish his work halfway but saves us really and completely. He does not rest until, after pronouncing his acquittal in our conscience, he has also imparted full holiness and glory to us. . . . [Evangelical sanctification] consists in the reality that in Christ God grants us, along with righteousness, also complete holiness, and does not just impute it but also inwardly imparts it by the regenerating and renewing working of the Holy Spirit until we have been fully conformed to the image of his Son.[16]

In other words, our doctrine of holiness must never be divorced from who Christ is and what he actually came to do. He came to die in order to make us holy (1 Pet. 2:24).

Justification answers to God's righteousness; sanctification answers to his holiness. "Hence, the two are equally necessary and are proclaimed in Scripture with equal emphasis. . . . Justification and sanctification . . . grant the same benefits," namely, "the entire Christ."[17]

God, the Holy One, imparts his holiness to Christ, who then works his image in his people by bestowing on them the Spirit of Christ. This is true Christian holiness.

22

GOD IS FAITHFUL

The steadfast love of the LORD never ceases;
   his mercies never come to an end;
they are new every morning;
   great is your faithfulness.

Lamentations 3:22–23

Doctrine

We can never take God's faithfulness for granted, especially since we live in a world filled with unfaithfulness. God is faithful: "Know therefore that the LORD your God is God, the faithful God who keeps covenant and steadfast love with those who love him and keep his commandments, to a thousand generations" (Deut. 7:9).

God abounds with all good things, such as truth. The denotation *the true and living God* (Jer. 10:10) does not indicate quite the same concept as the phrase "God is true" (John 3:33; cf. Rom. 3:4). The former has in view the existence of one God, the only God, but the latter communicates that this one God is a truthful God—a faithful God.

God is faithful because what he speaks is true; he cannot lie. We can count on him to remain devoted and loyal to his word and his very nature. God's faithfulness provides the basis for the "hope of eternal life, which God, who never lies, promised before the ages began" (Titus 1:2). Thus, his faithfulness is the very ground of our Christian religion. His people therefore set forth this praise: "Great is your faithfulness" (Lam. 3:23).

God's faithfulness toward us springs forth from his faithfulness to himself. When he speaks a promise to us, his character is on the line. To break a promise to us would be to deny himself: "If we are faithless, he remains faithful—for he cannot deny himself" (2 Tim. 2:13). God's people, even as unfaithful people, have always depended on God's faithfulness, especially against their enemies. Isaiah speaks of this in moving language:

> The LORD of hosts has sworn:
> "As I have planned,
>   so shall it be,
> and as I have purposed,
>   so shall it stand. . . ."
>
> For the LORD of hosts has purposed,
>   and who will annul it?
> His hand is stretched out,
>   and who will turn it back? (Isa. 14:24, 27)

God's faithfulness makes his decrees sure. Indeed, all his attributes presuppose his faithfulness. God remains unchangeable, holy, wise, good, eternal, omnipotent, and so forth, and therefore, he cannot but be faithful in what he says and how he acts. Denying God's faithfulness means denying him.

God proves to us his faithfulness through a covenant relationship with his people that he initiates. Each of his covenants includes promises and sometimes threats. Hence he speaks of his faithfulness in Deuteronomy 7:9–10 in terms of "keep[ing] covenant" with his people and showing them "steadfast love," yet also of repaying the wicked. Before that, he had revealed himself to Adam in the context of a covenant (i.e., the covenant of works).

All true theology finds its basis in some form of a divine covenant. True theology involves our understanding of God and necessarily manifests itself as relational theology, which is never meant to be simply cognitive, abstract, or disconnected from the God it reveals. The covenant bridges the great chasm between an infinite God and finite humanity. This covenantal relationship begins, however, in eternity between the three persons of the Trinity, which provides the ground for his faithfulness in his covenantal dealings with his people.

The eternal covenant of redemption has been understood as an agreement between the Father, Son, and Spirit for the redemption of sinners. Using anthropomorphic language, we may say that the Son "struck hands" with the Father concerning our redemption (Psalm 89). This covenant between the persons of the Trinity is, to use Thomas Goodwin's language, "the greatest affair, between persons of the highest sovereignty and majesty, that ever was transacted either in heaven or earth, or ever will be."[1]

The Father sent the Son and in so doing promised him glory and rewards. Christ had to rely on the faithfulness of God as much and more than we do, given the monumental work he performed. Indeed, in the midst of humiliation and suffering, Christ knew that his Father would be faithful to the promises he had made to the Son before the foundation of the world.

In Isaiah 49, we have what Thomas Goodwin calls a "most elegant Dialogue" between the Father and the Son in which the Father promises not just the Jews but also the Gentiles as a great reward (Isa. 49:6).[2] John 17 is the New Testament counterpart to Isaiah 49. Because Christ fulfilled the terms of the covenant to the satisfaction of the Father, he speaks in John 17:5 of his promised glory: "And now, Father, glorify me in your own presence with the glory that I had with you before the world existed." Such glory involves the Father bestowing on the elect faith, sanctification, and glory. The salvation of those given to Christ rests on the Father's faithfulness to the promises made to Jesus, which assures his people of his equal faithfulness to them.

Christ understood this. He was able to promise eternal life because he knew this promise firsthand from the Father, who gave it in the first place:

> And this is the will of him who sent me, that I should lose nothing of all that he has given me, but raise it up on the last day. For this is the will of my Father, that everyone who looks on the Son and believes in him should have eternal life, and I will raise him up on the last day. (John 6:39–40)

> I give them eternal life, and they will never perish, and no one will snatch them out of my hand. My Father, who has given them to me, is greater than all, and no one is able to snatch them out of the Father's hand. I and the Father are one. (John 10:28–30)

In these passages, the Father and the Son as two persons have but one will and purpose between them: to save sinners. Such oneness exists not only in their essence as God but also in their will and mind. Christ can make claims about salvation because he and the Father share the same desire. Moreover, the promises the Father makes to the Son include blessings not only for him but also for the elect.

Christ's Faithfulness

As the representative of the Father, Christ provides a living picture of God's faithfulness. He is called "Faithful and True" (Rev. 19:11) and is described in Isaiah as faithfully bringing forth justice (Isa. 42:3): "Righteousness shall be the belt of his waist, and faithfulness the belt of his loins" (Isa. 11:5).

As the way, the truth, and the life (John 14:6), Christ must be faithful, and he showed his faithfulness on earth by constantly obeying his Father's will (Luke 2:49; John 5:30; 6:38; 8:29; 14:31; Heb. 3:2). He was fully aware of his faithfulness as well: "I glorified you on earth, having accomplished the work that you gave me to do" (John 17:4).

Not only are all of God's words true (Ps. 119:43, 89–90; John 17:17), but also Jesus as God's mouthpiece declares and honors such truth. He promises both to be present where two or three are gathered in his name (Matt. 18:20) and to be with his disciples for all time (Matt. 28:20). His faithfulness to us is a matter of life and death: his life, death, and resurrected life. For this reason, we can rely on him concerning his promises about eternal life: "Truly, truly, I say to you, whoever hears my word and believes him who sent me has eternal life. He does not come into judgment, but has passed from death to life" (John 5:24).

We know Jesus must be faithful toward us because to qualify as a high priest, he had to show not only mercy but also faithfulness: "Therefore he had to be made like his brothers in every respect, so that he might become a merciful and faithful high priest in the service of God, to make propitiation for the sins of the people" (Heb. 2:17). According to John Owen, such faithfulness consists in his "exact, constant, careful consideration" of all our spiritual concerns, especially in our temptations and sufferings.[3] As a faithful high priest, he remains more concerned than we are about maintaining us in a state of grace. His faithfulness, not ours, guarantees our inheritance in the heavenly places with him.

Application

We are called to faithfulness ourselves. Our faith answers to God's faithfulness: "By faith Sarah herself received power to conceive, even when she was past the age, since she considered him faithful who had promised" (Heb. 11:11). As those who possess the Holy Spirit, we must exhibit faithfulness as the fruit of the Spirit (Gal. 5:22).

God considers our faithfulness something very significant. Indeed, to the church in Smyrna, Christ said, "Do not fear what you are about to suffer. Behold, the devil is about to throw some of you into prison, that you may be tested, and for ten days you will have tribulation. Be faithful unto death, and I will give you the crown of life" (Rev. 2:10).

Because Jesus himself conquered the Devil and death (Heb. 2:14), thus proving his own faithfulness, Christians can be faithful in the midst of trials and persecutions. Such faithfulness would be utterly impossible apart from God showing his own faithfulness through Christ. So in light of the grand realities of the gospel, we can and must be faithful. Faithfulness that endures in all sorts of circumstances remains the path that leads to glory. The apostle John stands before us as one such person who endured in difficult circumstances (Rev. 1:9).

Faithfulness toward God and Christ in light of their faithfulness toward us provides the ground of faithfulness toward others in this life. The vertical leads to the horizontal.

In marriage, so much is made of love, but too little is made of faithful love. Christian love is faithful because the fruit of the Spirit does not allow us to pick and choose which graces we wish to possess. We bear them all or none at all in the Christian life.

If faithful pastors were asked what they wish from church members, they would very quickly mention faithfulness. We do not require that people possess the power and devotion of David, the wisdom and wealth of Solomon, or the gifts and sanctification of Paul. We simply want our people to be faithful in their service of the King. Not brilliant, rich, or powerful, but faithful.

As we have seen, God is holy and merciful and desires his children to be the same. Likewise, God is faithful and desires that his children resemble, by the power of the Holy Spirit, the Father and the Son in their faithfulness.

23

GOD IS GRACIOUS

The LORD is merciful and gracious,
  slow to anger and abounding in
    steadfast love.
He will not always chide,
  nor will he keep his anger forever.
He does not deal with us according to our sins,
  nor repay us according to our iniquities.
For as high as the heavens are above the earth,
  so great is his steadfast love toward those who
    fear him;
as far as the east is from the west,
  so far does he remove our transgressions
    from us.
As a father shows compassion to his children,
  so the LORD shows compassion to those who
    fear him.
For he knows our frame;
  he remembers that we are dust.

Psalm 103:8–14

Doctrine

The Bible clearly identifies God as gracious:

> But you, O Lord, are a God merciful and gracious,
>> slow to anger and abounding in steadfast love and
>>> faithfulness. (Ps. 86:15)

> The LORD is gracious and merciful,
>> slow to anger and abounding in steadfast love.
> The LORD is good to all,
>> and his mercy is over all that he has made. (Ps. 145:8–9)

Generally speaking, God's grace denotes his tendency to freely show favor to creatures who do not deserve it. In considering grace as expressed by God in Scripture, we speak of his common and special grace. Leigh treats these distinct yet overlapping expressions of God's grace:

1. Commonly, when he exercises beneficence and liberality towards all creatures, pouring upon them plentifully all goods of nature, body, mind, and fortune, so that there is nothing which tastes not of the inexhaustible fountain of his blessings and goodness (Matt. 5:44–45; Ps. 36:5–6).
2. Specially, toward the church, by which he bestows eternal life on certain men fallen by sin, and redeemed in Christ (Titus 2:11; 3:4).[1]

With this pattern in mind, God's grace toward his creatures may be understood not only as his postfall response but also as his basic mode of relating to his creatures. He gives gifts to his creatures. Because God is gracious, he will relate to his creatures, made in his image, by way of grace. This does not deny that his grace has different aspects, but it does mean that no one can say that God has not been gracious to some degree.

Did Adam receive any "graces" in the garden? Was God gracious to Adam even before he fell into sin? Yes. God must necessarily be gracious in his dealings with humanity. He is gracious, and he expresses such grace in both his attitude toward us and his relationship with us.

Historically, the (heretical) Socinians spoke of Adam's natural innocence, but they denied that he had any infused graces or habits of holiness. In their view, then, God did not relate to Adam in grace in any way whatsoever. At the other extreme, Roman Catholics have typically argued that *all* of Adam's holiness was supernatural (i.e., the superadded gift), a view that actually undermines grace. Trying to stay a middle course, most Reformed theologians have argued that the image of God was natural to Adam but that this did not mean that God gave no superadded grace at all to him in the garden of Eden.

In the garden, Adam and Eve were not immutably holy. They were liable to both temptation and sin. As a dependent creature, Adam was not allowed to trust in his own powers, even in Eden. To do that would be to rebel against God. Therefore, John Owen makes the point that Adam's true fault in the garden was a failure to trust in the Holy Spirit to sustain him.[2]

Thomas Goodwin also makes a similar argument: the Holy Spirit "was in Adam's heart to assist his graces, and cause them to flow and bring forth, and to move him to live according to those principles of life given him."[3] Yet Christians "have the Spirit upon Christ's account, in his name, purchased by him, as whom he had first received, also purchased as the head of the church."[4] The giving of the Holy Spirit to Adam was not earned by him but was rather a result of God's free gift (grace).

The learned Puritan Francis Roberts, author of the largest work on covenant theology in the English language, contends that grace in Scripture "has manifold acceptations."[5] Primarily, grace refers to God's free favor to his creatures and the blessings he gives to them. In the covenant of works, Adam received the grace of benevolence; in the covenant of grace, he received the grace of mercy.

In the covenant of grace, we receive "superabounding" grace

because it comes through Christ's death and resurrection. God gives us the opposite of what we deserve. In Ephesians 2, Paul speaks of God being "rich in mercy" (v. 4). As such, because of his "great love" toward us (v. 4), he makes spiritually dead people alive in Christ (v. 5), in order to "show the immeasurable riches of his grace in kindness toward us in Christ Jesus" (v. 7). Thus, we have been saved "by grace"—not by our own doing but because of the "gift of God" (v. 8). If it were of our works, we could boast (v. 9), but even our good works have been prepared by God "beforehand, that we should walk in them" (v. 10). This is what is meant, then, by the grace of God in Christ.

God's Grace to Christ[6]

Because God is gracious, should we expect him to be gracious to Christ? If so, then surely we can argue that God's grace is not only goodness shown in the place of demerit. In fact, the Father upheld his Son, his servant, by bestowing on him the Holy Spirit to enable him to perform his appointed work (Isa. 42:1). The gracious gift of the enabling Spirit flows from the terms of the eternal covenant of redemption.

In Luke's Gospel, we read of Christ, "And the child grew and became strong, filled with wisdom. And the favor [Gk. *charis*] of God was upon him. . . . And Jesus increased in wisdom and in stature and in favor [Gk. *chariti*] with God and man" (Luke 2:40, 52).

Luke speaks of Jesus increasing in *chariti* (from the Gk. *charis*). Does this term mean "favor," as many English translations suggest? Or should we translate the Greek as "grace"? A number of translations render *charis* in Luke 2:40 as "grace" (e.g., NASB, NIV, KJV). We need not get too picky about which word is used provided we understand that divine grace is not merely his goodness to the elect in the era of redemptive history or something only offered to those who have sinned.

Divine grace is a perfection of God's nature and thus a characteristic of how he relates to finite creatures, even apart from sin.

In the garden, the grace of God came to Adam; in the wilderness, grace was showered on his Son, the second Adam. God could be "gracious" to Jesus, not as though Jesus sinned but simply because God is a grace-giving God—and if he shows grace to his creatures, how much more to his beloved Son? God showed favor to his favorite Son. Christ's human nature was sanctified and filled with graces (Gal. 5:22).

According to John Owen, "For let the natural faculties of the soul, mind, will, and affections, be created pure, innocent, undefiled,—as they cannot be otherwise created immediately by God,—yet there is not enough to enable any rational creature to live to God; much less was it all that was in Jesus Christ."[7] Similarly, Bavinck argues, "If humans in general cannot have communion with God except by the Holy Spirit, then this applies even more powerfully to Christ's human nature."[8]

Quite apart from Luke 2:40, 52, we have the example of Philippians 2:9. There Paul uses the Greek word *echarisato*. The same Greek word appears earlier in Philippians 1:29, where believers are "freely/graciously given" the privilege of both believing in and suffering for Christ. The kindness and goodness of God are revealed in the gracious gift he bestows on Christ. There exists no unworthiness in Christ, as though God had to show mercy to him, but that does not keep God from being gracious (by way of granting gifts) to his beloved Son.

Application

Every Christian can and must confess with the apostle Paul, "By the grace of God I am what I am" (1 Cor. 15:10). This well-known verse shows that God's grace is not merely a "get out of jail free" card that allows us to behave in any way we wish.

This is the tragedy of much thinking about God's grace today. Notice that Paul goes on to say, "And his grace toward me was not in vain. On the contrary, I worked harder than any of them, though it was not I, but the grace of God that is with me" (1 Cor. 15:10).

He affirms that he worked harder than others only by the grace of God. Grace works.

God bestows many gifts on his children. They are all of grace. Some of these gifts are titles and privileges; others enable us to be diligent for the work of God's kingdom. But whatever we accomplish, we do so by the grace of God. Charles Spurgeon appropriately notes,

> When we put our foot upon the threshold of glory, and pass through the gate of pearl to the golden pavement of the heavenly city, the last step will be as much taken through the grace of God, as was the first step when we turned unto our great Father in our rags and misery. Left by the grace of God for a single moment, we would perish. We are dependent as much upon grace for spiritual life as we are upon the air we breathe for this natural life.[9]

Because of the grace of God, there exists absolutely no room for pride in the Christian life. None whatsoever. Speaking to the Corinthians, Paul says, "For who sees anything different in you? What do you have that you did not receive? If then you received it, why do you boast as if you did not receive it?" (1 Cor. 4:7).

The Scriptures never seem to tire of warning us that God's grace should inspire in us thankfulness, praise, and humility. Thus, Paul explains to the Romans, "For by the grace given to me I say to everyone among you not to think of himself more highly than he ought to think, but to think with sober judgment, each according to the measure of faith that God has assigned" (Rom. 12:3). John the Baptist similarly remarks, "A person cannot receive even one thing unless it is given him from heaven" (John 3:27).

Grace shown to us leads us to exercise our humility both before God (from whom every gift comes, James 1:17) and before man. We should show not envy toward others for the gifts God has seen fit to give them and not us but rather thankfulness that he has given anything at all. Our own gifts should prompt not pride in ourselves but humility toward God, who alone makes us to differ.

Apart from the grace of God, all our best efforts are like menstrual cloths before a holy God (Isa. 64:6). He finds and creates in us what is pleasing to him because he is gracious. If God showed grace to his beloved Son, who was made like us in every way except without sin, then how much more do we need grace? Such grace sustains us spiritually in the same way that the air sustains us physically.

24

GOD IS JUST

For according to the work of a man he will
repay him,
and according to his ways he will make it
befall him.
Of a truth, God will not do wickedly,
and the Almighty will not pervert justice.
Job 34:11–12

Doctrine

God is just; he is the essentially and incomparably Righteous One.
Even if Pharaoh was being disingenuous, we can still repeat his
words as our own (even corporately): "This time I have sinned;
the LORD is in the right, and I and my people are in the wrong"
(Ex. 9:27). God's people should love to confess his justice as much
as his love, for his love is his justice, and his justice is his love:

> The Rock, his work is perfect,
>   for all his ways are justice.
> A God of faithfulness and without iniquity,
>   just and upright is he. (Deut. 32:4)

Abraham also recognized this truth when he interceded for
Sodom in light of God's impending destruction of the city: "Far be

185

it from you to do such a thing, to put the righteous to death with
the wicked, so that the righteous fare as the wicked! Far be that
from you! Shall not the Judge of all the earth do what is just?"
(Gen. 18:25).

According to Edward Leigh, there are five categories that help
us to understand and prove the justice of God:

1. Affirmatively, when it calls him Just, a Revenger, Holy, Right,
   and extols his Justice (Ex. 9:27; Ps. 11:7; Jer. 12:1).
2. Negatively, when it removes from him injustice and iniquity,
   respect of persons, and receiving of gifts, and also the causes
   and effects of injustice (Deut. 32:4; 10:17; Dan. 9:14; Job 8:3).
3. Affectively, when it attributes to him zeal, anger, fury (Ex.
   20:5; 32:10; Num. 11:10), which are not in God such passions
   as they be in us, but an act of the immutable justice.
4. Symbolically, when it calls him a consuming fire (Deut. 4:24);
   compares him to an angry Lion, an armed soldier (Isa. 38:13;
   [42:13]).
5. Effectively, when it affirms that he renders to everyone according to his works (1 Sam. 26:23).[1]

Because God is holy, he must also be just. Holiness stands in
complete opposition to sin, and justice displays such opposition.
This we call his retributive justice. Those who have seen much evil
in their lives cherish the justice of God as exceedingly precious, for
they know that he will righteously repay the wicked:

God is a righteous judge,
  and a God who feels indignation every day.

If a man does not repent, God will whet his sword;
  he has bent and readied his bow;
he has prepared for him his deadly weapons,
  making his arrows fiery shafts. (Ps. 7:11–13)

With that in mind, God loves holiness in others and also exercises his remunerative justice, which is quite prominent in Scripture.

This form of justice deals out rewards in response to the righteous acts of people. God's justice must be understood, then, in public, not private, terms. Thus the Scriptures are frequently speaking of his justice in relation to the actions of men. So after sparing Saul's life, David declares, "The LORD rewards every man for his righteousness and his faithfulness, for the LORD gave you into my hand today, and I would not put out my hand against the LORD's anointed" (1 Sam. 26:23).

God's remunerative and retributive justice may be understood clearly from the creation account. God's relationship with Adam in the garden was covenantal, and according to his justice, when he instituted a covenant with Adam, God faithfully enabled man to commune with him and fulfill the obligations of the covenant. God's righteousness demands that when he created all things good, he endowed Adam with the ability to enjoy God's goodness.

Since God is the righteous, holy, and good Creator, he does for his creatures what is worthy of the Creator-creature relationship. He was under no obligation to exceed what his position required as Creator. He gave Adam and Eve all that they needed to attain to happiness, and they could never accuse him of injustice if they failed to fulfill their covenant obligations. As long as Adam and Eve continued in obedience, God was righteously bound in covenant to continue his favor toward them.

Though God, by virtue of his righteousness, bound himself to certain covenantal "dues" to his creatures, he was not obliged to preserve his creatures in their state of innocence. Adam failed, not God. In God's goodness, he remains just. Yet the way he treats his creatures in justice does not mean that he does not also treat them well, as evidenced in the case of Adam and Eve.

The Necessity of Christ's Death

As a just God, everything he ordains is just. He never gives his creatures less than they deserve, though he can, because of his grace, give us more than we deserve. We might rightly ask, how can a just God give us more than we deserve, since we are sinners? Simply, the satisfaction of Christ on the cross shows God to be both just and merciful.

Theologians over the centuries have wrestled with the difficult question whether God could have forgiven sin as a mere act of his will apart from the satisfaction of Christ. Was his death absolutely necessary to save sinners?

In the seventeenth century, John Owen ably set forth the position that Christ's death was necessary for God to save sinners, but several of his contemporaries, including William Twisse, Thomas Goodwin, and Samuel Rutherford (all of whom were present at the Westminster Assembly), were of a different persuasion. They argued that God, by a free act of his will, could have pardoned sin apart from the death of Christ. While the arguments made by both sides are complex and beyond the scope of this volume, a brief discussion will help us see what's at stake.

We can say that God's decision to create the world was free, not necessary. But in creating the world, he could not divorce his attributes from the manner in which he created. Thus, he created omnipotently because he is the all-powerful God.

In the same way, because God is essentially just, he must punish sin as the one who also immutably hates it. In order to eternally preserve his glory and do justice to himself (and to humanity), he of necessity renders judgment on sin. As the holy God with absolute dominion, he cannot allow hatred of his holy being; he must punish it. God loves his own being, which is to say that he loves justice and the exercise of it.

As a result, to pardon sinners, God demands satisfaction. In Anselm's famous work *Cur Deus Homo?* (Why did God become man?), he answers the question based on the justice and honor of God. God became man because man owed him a debt, a debt so large that only God could pay it—hence the God-man, Jesus Christ.

Modifying Anselm's approach slightly, theologians centuries

later argued that the death of Christ demonstrates the essential justice of God. For example, Francis Turretin maintains,

> For if it was free and indifferent to God to punish or not to punish sin without compromising his justice so that no reason besides the mere will impelled God to send his Son into the world to die for us, what lawful reason can be devised to account for God's willing to subject his most beloved and holy Son to an accursed and most cruel death?[2]

Turretin thus deemed it unacceptable that a wise and good God would "gratuitously" and "without the highest necessity" allow his Son to die on a cross, unless his justice demanded a sacrifice for sinners.[3] It is no wonder, then, that the book of Romans places a strong accent on the righteousness of God in saving sinners:

> But now the righteousness of God has been manifested apart from the law, although the Law and the Prophets bear witness to it—the righteousness of God through faith in Jesus Christ for all who believe. For there is no distinction: for all have sinned and fall short of the glory of God, and are justified by his grace as a gift, through the redemption that is in Christ Jesus, whom God put forward as a propitiation by his blood, to be received by faith. This was to show God's righteousness, because in his divine forbearance he had passed over former sins. It was to show his righteousness at the present time, so that he might be just and the justifier of the one who has faith in Jesus. (Rom. 3:21–26)

God is both just and the justifier of the wicked. He is both just and merciful. Who he is, he is to us in the way he saves us—and nothing less than that will do.

Patrick Gillespie states that through Christ, God's "glorious attributes and nature was made conspicuous, and the declarative glory thereof had a more glorious luster, than by all the works of Creation and Providence beside."[4] Gillespie's point has been a dominant theme throughout this book: nothing gives a greater display of God's attributes than his Son who became man.

Application

God's justice should be a source of great comfort to his people. There are many things we do not understand in this life because we are not God, yet in those times, God's justice reassures us.

For example, God often inflicts great sufferings on his people: "But if in spite of this you will not listen to me, but walk contrary to me, then I will walk contrary to you in fury, and I myself will discipline you sevenfold for your sins" (Lev. 26:27–28). Thomas Watson quotes Augustine as saying, "God's ways of judgment are sometimes secret, but never unjust."[5] Watson adds, "The trials and sufferings of the godly are to refine and purify them."[6] God never unjustly afflicts us.

But the glory of the Christian religion may be seen in the fact that when we are stricken, we can continually affirm the justice of God simultaneously with his mercy, wisdom, grace, goodness, and the rest of his attributes. He only ever acts toward us in a manner consistent with his whole being.

God tempers his afflictions—mercy!

God uses our afflictions to make us like his Son—wisdom!

God does not entice us to sin in our afflictions—holiness!

God brings us afflictions to keep us from hell—goodness!

Because God is eminently just in pardoning our sin through Christ, he is also exceptionally merciful, wise, holy, and good toward us. The blessings that we receive were purchased not by us but for us by Christ. We are simply beggars who receive the rewards freely from the hand of our just God. His merit leads to our gift.

But for the impenitent, apart from Christ there remains only justice. That is also a source of comfort to us who believe. We who see all the unpunished evil in this world can take comfort from the fact that God is not unjust. He will repay each person according to his deeds. When the psalmist "discerned" the end of the wicked, all the evil he observed made sense; he could glory in having God as his "portion" and in seeing how good it was to "be near" to him (Ps. 73:17, 26–28). Paul makes clear that God's just judgment will surely come:

> The times of ignorance God overlooked, but now he commands all people everywhere to repent, because he has fixed a day on which he will judge the world in righteousness by a man whom he has appointed; and of this he has given assurance to all by raising him from the dead. (Acts 17:30–31)

God judges the world in righteousness through his Son. The resurrection of Christ proves that God is just, for he promised Christ that he would not let him see decay (Acts 2:22–34). But the resurrection also grants to him an authority to judge those outside him. Watson remarks,

> Now things are out of course; sin is rampant, saints are wronged, they are often cast in a righteous cause, they can meet with no justice here, justice is turned into wormwood; but there is a day coming, when God will set things right; he will do every man justice; he will crown the righteous and condemn the wicked. . . . If God be a just God, he will take vengeance. God has given men a law to live by, and they break it. There must be a day for the execution of offenders. A law not executed is but like a wooden dagger, for a show. At the last day, God's sword shall be drawn out against offenders; then his justice shall be revealed before all the world. . . . The wicked shall drink a sea of wrath, but not sip one drop of injustice. At that day shall all mouths be stopped, and God's justice shall be fully vindicated from all the cavils and clamours of unjust men.[7]

The fact of God's justice and the certainty of its execution extend some comfort when we are so grieved by the wickedness of man in this world. Indeed, because justice remains essential to God, we are to love him as much for his justice as for any other attribute. When he destroys the wicked in the life to come, we shall be eminently but never cruelly pleased with his works of judgment.

25

GOD IS ANGRY

Now therefore let me alone, that my wrath may burn
hot against them and I may consume them, in order
that I may make a great nation of you.

Exodus 32:10

Doctrine

God's anger, wrath, fury, and hatred represent the negative side of
his justice and holiness. He hates and therefore punishes all that
is opposed to his holy nature. This theme features prominently
in both the Old and New Testaments (e.g., Pss. 69:24; 76:10; Jer.
21:14; John 3:36; Rom. 1:18; Rev. 19:15).

Yet we must be exceedingly careful when discussing this attribute, because of the doctrine of impassibility, the idea that our immutable God exists without passions. His infinite and immutable
blessedness means that he does not experience change in his divine
essence. Our actions cannot inflict suffering or distress on him,
which his glory will not allow. Hence, when the Scriptures speak
of God as angry or jealous, we must understand these emotions as
metaphors or anthropopathisms (i.e., human feelings figuratively
applied to God). He may "assume" such descriptions of himself in
order to accommodate to us in our weakness as creatures.

God reveals his anger through acts of his outward will toward creatures. By an external and constant act of his will, God hates sin and inflicts punishment on sinners. William Ames affirms that when Scripture attributes affections such as hatred to God, these "either designate acts of the will or apply to God only figuratively."[1] Some Reformed theologians consider anger a proper and essential virtue of God's nature, but I think Ames's view is safest and best. Simply put, God's anger remains an expression of his outward will, not his essential being.

Impenitent sinners who reject God are the objects of his general and temporal anger: "For the wrath of God is revealed from heaven against all ungodliness and unrighteousness of men, who by their unrighteousness suppress the truth" (Rom. 1:18). Sin necessarily elicits God's wrath: ". . . immorality, impurity, passion, evil desire, and covetousness, which is idolatry. On account of these the wrath of God is coming" (Col. 3:5–6).

In the Old Testament are numerous examples of God's wrath on the wicked. Consider these solemn yet magnificent words against Nineveh:

> The LORD is a jealous and avenging God;
>> the LORD is avenging and wrathful;
> the LORD takes vengeance on his adversaries
>> and keeps wrath for his enemies.
> The LORD is slow to anger and great in power,
>> and the LORD will by no means clear the guilty.
> His way is in whirlwind and storm,
>> and the clouds are the dust of his feet.
> He rebukes the sea and makes it dry;
>> he dries up all the rivers;
> Bashan and Carmel wither;
>> the bloom of Lebanon withers.
> The mountains quake before him;
>> the hills melt;
> the earth heaves before him,
>> the world and all who dwell in it.

Who can stand before his indignation?
    Who can endure the heat of his anger?
His wrath is poured out like fire,
    and the rocks are broken into pieces by him. (Nah. 1:2–6)

Moreover, by flooding the world during Noah's time, God showed that he did not take sin lightly. As Bavinck attests, "This wrath is terrible (Ps. 76:7), inspires dread (Ps. 2:5; 90:7), brings pain (Job 21:17; Ps. 102:10), punishment (Ps. 6:1; 38:1; Jer. 10:24), and destruction (Jer. 42:18)."[2] Moreover, God's wrathful judgment "will only reveal itself in all its power in the future, in the day of wrath (Deut. 32:41–42; Ps. 94:1, 149:7, Isa. 34:8, 35:4, 59:17; 61:2, 4; Jer. 46:10)."[3]

The fact of hell as a place of eternal punishment reveals the anger of God. For those who do not obey the gospel "will suffer the punishment of eternal destruction, away from the presence of the Lord and from the glory of his might" (2 Thess. 1:9).

God will judge the wicked in the unquenchable fire of hell, where their worm (e.g., that which devours or torments) never dies (Mark 9:44–48). Those outside Christ will be bound hand and foot and taken away into outer darkness, where they will weep and gnash their teeth (Matt. 22:13). Joseph was cast into a pit (Gen. 37:24), while Paul and Silas were cast into a prison (Acts 16:23), but Christ will cast the wicked into a "pit" of hell, where they will be confined for all eternity. Nebuchadnezzar's fiery furnace would be ice compared with the heat of God's wrath.

Another type of God's anger that we need to consider is that expressed toward the elect. God indeed expresses anger toward Christians, contrary to what some believe today. Affirming this reality has important pastoral implications, especially that God can and does punish his people for their sins. The Westminster Confession of Faith affirms the scriptural teaching that even though believers cannot lose their justification, they can fall under God's fatherly displeasure: "Yet they may, by their sins, fall under God's fatherly displeasure, and not have the light of his countenance restored unto them, until they humble themselves, confess their sins, beg pardon, and renew their faith and repentance" (11.5).

Still, when speaking of the fatherly displeasure of God, we need to make a qualification. God vindictively punishes the impenitent, but he castigates his children out of fatherly love. Even in the latter case, God expresses displeasure with their sin and inflicts the pain of discipline for their good (Heb. 12:4–11). For example, after sinning in a most grotesque manner against Bathsheba and Uriah, David fell under God's displeasure: "But the thing that David had done displeased the LORD" (2 Sam. 11:27). Second Samuel chronicles all the consequences of David's sins. We may be forgiven by God, but the painful consequences and judgments of the Lord are not always removed.

Christ's Anger

God's anger, expressed without passions, does not perturb his being. But while on earth, Christ experienced the passion of anger, albeit sinless anger. He was vexed in his spirit because, as a true human being, he could not be emotionally and thus physically indifferent to sin and hardness of heart (Mark 3:5). If Christ had not expressed anger in the presence of injustice, he would not have been godly. It is impossible for a holy human to be unaffected by sin. Having the mind of God, Christ brought glory to his Father in the way he reacted to every situation he encountered. As such, whatever would cause God to be angry (in terms of an expression of his outward will) also caused Christ to respond in anger.

For example, after asking the Jews whether it was lawful to heal on the Sabbath, they remained silent. This provoked Christ: "And he looked around at them with anger, grieved at their hardness of heart" (Mark 3:5). Christ could show mercy and express anger because the situation demanded it. These impenitent sinners deserved to be rebuked and punished for such wickedness.

And they received the most solemn form of earthly punishment: hardness of heart. God can show his anger not only by refusing grace to the impenitent but also by actively hardening their hearts according to his secret will and purposes.

But not only with the impenitent was Christ angry. He showed anger even toward his own beloved disciples. As children were brought to Jesus in order for him to bless them, the disciples acted contrary to the compassion of Christ, rebuking the people for bringing their children to him. Jesus "was indignant" (Mark 10:14). Christ also cleared the temple on two occasions (Mark 11:15–19; John 2:13–17), acting zealously for his Father's honor with great moral and physical strength.

Likewise, we need to exercise righteous anger. This may be one of the most difficult passions for us to exercise in a godly manner, but that does not mean that we should not, as Spirit-filled Christians, get angry when the occasion demands that we get angry for God's glory.

We see the anger of God not only in Christ but also on him in his death. In the words of Thomas Goodwin, "That God should put to death his own Son for sin, when he became but a surety for it, was a clearer manifestation of his anger, and a higher piece of justice against sin, than if he had made and there sacrificed millions of worlds."[4]

Christ understood holy anger better than anyone. No wonder, then, that he was terrified at the prospect of the cross, where the anger of God would be unleashed on him like a torrent, as he took our place of punishment. It was a fearful thing for Christ to fall into the hands of the living God precisely because he perfectly understood such anger from the vantage point of his own purity and holiness.

Application

"It is a fearful thing to fall into the hands of the living God" (Heb. 10:31). Throughout the book of Hebrews, the author issues warnings like this one to his readers several times and in various ways. Should believers fear God as a Father in terms of his ability and willingness to punish them? In fact, we would be impious if we did not. This in no way takes away from the Father's love for his children. We can understand this thinking from an earthly perspective: small children with full assurance of their dad's affection toward them can still fear him for the discipline he will bring for their disobedience or disrespect. They fear him not as slaves who run from their master but as children who find refuge in the very one who administers the discipline.

In the garden of Eden, a context without sin and with only a loving relationship between a Father (God) and his son (Adam), the former still warned the latter that he would face judgment if he ate from the forbidden tree (Gen. 2:17). When God confronted Adam in his sin, the man responded, "I heard the sound of you in the garden, and I was afraid, because I was naked, and I hid myself" (Gen. 3:10). It would have been impious of Adam to strut around the garden as if he had nothing to worry about after sinning so egregiously against a loving Father. Therefore, God's warning in the garden proves that he will be angry with sin. Adam's response was actually appropriate to the situation.

Christ warns that those who do not bear fruit will be cut off: "If anyone does not abide in me he is thrown away like a branch and withers; and the branches are gathered, thrown into the fire, and burned" (John 15:6). Paul similarly warns Gentiles, who have been engrafted into Israel, not to be proud: "That is true. They were broken off because of their unbelief, but you stand fast through faith. So do not become proud, but fear. For if God did not spare the natural branches, neither will he spare you" (Rom. 11:20–21). Paul also warns the Corinthians about God's judgment on his people, particularly calling those who think they stand to take heed lest they fall (1 Cor. 10:12). And the author of Hebrews warns against unbelief (Hebrews 3–4) and later against the forsaking of assembling together (Heb. 10:25–31).

Thus, as Christians, we cannot simply think of God's judgment as something that in no way applies to us. It is true, indeed, that there is no condemnation for those of us who are in Christ Jesus (Rom. 8:1). But God's people cannot live presumptuously. We cannot openly rebel against God. The Christian who decides to follow a course of action that brazenly violates God's law can expect severe fatherly discipline.

One way in which we escape such judgment is to look daily to Christ, the pioneer and perfecter of our faith (Heb. 12:2). We run with endurance, along with other believers, in order to win the prize (Phil. 3:14). We also must fear the Lord with a reverential fear:

> The LORD takes pleasure in those who fear him,
> in those who hope in his steadfast love. (Ps. 147:11)

God delights in our godly fear of him. We consider who he is, and we live before him in reverent fear, which actually keeps us from having to fear the awesome judgments of God. When Christians lose the fear of God by failing to take him seriously, it is at those times that they actually need to fear him most. We have two choices: to live in reverent fear of God because of his awesome and holy name or to fear his temporal and eternal judgments on us because we have chosen to regard him as unworthy of our lifelong adoration. After all, if our Savior's prayers were heard because of his reverence (Heb. 5:7), then should we not also live in the fear of God?

26

GOD IS ANTHROPOMORPHIC

Look down from heaven and see,
from your holy and beautiful habitation.
Where are your zeal and your might?
The stirring of your inner parts and your
compassion
are held back from me.
For you are our Father,
though Abraham does not know us,
and Israel does not acknowledge us;
you, O LORD, are our Father,
our Redeemer from of old is your name.
O LORD, why do you make us wander from
your ways
and harden our heart, so that we fear you not?
Return for the sake of your servants,
the tribes of your heritage.
Your holy people held possession for a little while;
our adversaries have trampled down your sanctuary.
We have become like those over whom you have
never ruled,
like those who are not called by your name.

Isaiah 63:15–19

Doctrine

Almost all that pertains to humans in the Scriptures is also attributed to God. The Bible speaks of God's "face" (Ex. 33:20), "eyes" and "eyelids" (Ps. 11:4), "ear" (Isa. 59:1), "nostrils" (Isa. 65:5), "mouth" (Deut. 8:3), "lips" (Isa. 30:27), "tongue" (Isa. 30:27), "finger" (Ex. 8:19), and many others body parts. Additionally, human emotions are ascribed to God. His people grieve him at times (Ps. 78:40; Isa. 63:10), he says that he "regretted" making humanity (Gen. 6:6), and he sometimes expresses jealousy and anger (Deut. 32:21).

Many passages in God's Word ascribe "passions" to God. Yet the Westminster Confession of Faith affirms from Scripture that God is "without passions" (2.1). The Westminster divines held to a view that God is impassible ("without passions") because they viewed him as unchangeable. Almost all seventeenth-century Reformed theologians left out the concept of impassibility when discussing the attributes of God but not because they thought it unimportant. Instead, they spoke of his immutability, which implies that he does not (and cannot) have passions.

By suggesting that God is impassible, Reformed theologians have argued that nothing inside or outside him can cause suffering or distress. Immutability asserts the same thing as impassibility but in more appropriate language. No external agent can affect God to the point that he changes in his being.

Reformed theologians speak of God having divine virtues or affections. Affections such as wrath or hatred are either acts of God's outward will, or they are applied to God only figuratively, not properly. As Richard Muller says,

> The affections are, therefore, either inward and inalterable dispositions of the divine will or figurative attributions based on *ad extra* manifestations. Furthermore, what makes an attribution of an affection to God figurative or metaphorical is its apparent variation, temporality, or alterability.[1]

Affections in God are not the same as affections in humans. Divine affections do not refer to changes in God's essence. They are permanent dispositions. Thus, affections are distinct from passions. Muller distinguishes between affections and passions in the following way:

> An affection is usually favorable or positive, whereas a passion is usually negative. . . . A passion, most strictly, is a form of suffering and would not have the connotation of a permanent disposition. . . . Passions . . . indicate a declension from an original or natural condition that is at variance with the fundamental inclination of the individual—and, therefore, a loss of power or self-control.[2]

Passions, then, refer to an internal emotional change in relation to something outside itself. Very simply, human beings cannot make God less happy in himself. Not only would he then be changeable, but also he would not be infinitely blessed. Since God knows all things eternally (and thus infallibly), he cannot "respond" to events in a way that either surprises or grieves him. In no way is God subject to his creatures. He is the infinite Creator; we are the finite creatures.

For God to experience passions would mean that God changes. The passion of anger, for example, is the acquiring of one quality, rage, by losing another, peace (or joy). God cannot lose his infinite blessedness, so when we speak of the anger of God, we do so only figuratively (or "improperly"). Anger is an affection of the divine will toward evil.

With that in mind, as noted previously, the Scriptures do speak of passions in God, such as anger, jealousy, and grief/repentance. These so-called passions in him are actually words that reflect the acts of his outward will and so are spoken of him metaphorically. If we grant that passions are attributed to him only metaphorically, then everything else that has been said about him in this book can stand in harmony. The unchangeable, eternal, powerful, blessed God is just that. If he is not impassible, though, then the whole doctrine of God as laid out by theologians over the course of church history completely falls apart, despite the best attempts of some to try and make God "passioned."

In John Owen's estimation, "A mutable god is of the dunghill."[3] The perfect, blessed God ceases to be God if his blessedness can be changed by some external agent, such as man or the Devil. If we can properly ascribe grief to God, then we deny him infinite blessedness, and he is to be pitied. May it never be.

The Scriptures speak abundantly of the anger, wrath, and fury of God (Num. 25:3–4; Deut. 13:17; 29:24; Josh. 7:26; Judg. 2:14; 2 Chron. 28:11; Ezra 10:14; Pss. 69:24; 74:1; 78:31, 49; Isa. 13:9; 30:30; 34:2; Lam. 2:6; Ezek. 5:15; Hab. 3:8, 12; Rom. 1:18). For example, Joshua 7 recounts the sin of Achan, which led to Israel's defeat at Ai. Once his iniquity was discovered, Achan was put to death. Joshua 7:26 concludes the story: "And they raised over him a great heap of stones that remains to this day. Then the LORD turned from his burning anger."

In this account, we have to ask whether God's "burning anger" is spoken properly of him in terms of his essence being changed by the sin of Achan, or whether this is a figurative expression, specifically an anthropopathism. When God wills for the wicked to be punished, sometimes in the severest way (e.g., the flood in Noah's time), we can speak of the "anger of the Lord." Because God is holy and righteous, he must punish sin. So when God outwardly executes his punishment, the Scriptures often speak of his fury or wrath, but this applies figuratively to God without impinging on his essential attributes (e.g., holiness, blessedness). To suggest, then, that Achan could upset God so that God is less happy is to make Achan into God and God into Achan.

Another question Scripture presents us with is, does the Lord have "regret"? The answer is yes and no. For example, 1 Samuel 15:29 states, "And also the Glory of Israel will not lie or have regret, for he is not a man, that he should have regret." In that same context, however, God is said to have regretted making Saul king (1 Sam. 15:11, 35). How can we reconcile these passages?

Benedict Pictet, echoing many Reformed theologians who have written on this topic, says,

> Repentance may apply to God, because he sometimes changes his work, and so far does the same thing which men do when they repent. . . . [T]his change of work does not imply a change in the mind of God, for by one and the same act of his will he decrees both to do the work, and afterwards to alter it; thus he did at the same time decree to create men and to destroy them all by a deluge ages after.[4]

Thus, God does not change with respect to his essence and character. But because we change, his interactions with us change. Those interactions reflect his never-changing character. God displays his immutability in his dynamic relations with mutable humanity. This is an important qualification. Merely employing the anthropomorphism scheme (i.e., proper vs. improper) can be too mechanical if we are not careful. That is, by ascribing anthropomorphic terms to God, Scripture reveals something real about him in his dealings with the world. We cannot escape the reality that God accommodates to us in his dealings with us. His love and wisdom demand accommodation.

God cannot be fully comprehended, even in what he chooses to reveal about himself to us. Nevertheless, what he reveals, as it comes to us in an understandable form, rests on divine truth. Our knowledge of him is from himself, through the Mediator, which finds its form in his Word. God thus accommodates himself to us by speaking through a Mediator. If he did not, we would not be able to understand him. God's names are just one example of God's condescension and accommodations to us. In fact, as Herman Bavinck notes, Scripture "does not just contain a few scattered anthropomorphisms but is anthropomorphic through and through."[5]

God relates to us in a way that does justice to the history of redemption. He condescends and, for our sake, sometimes appropriates to himself passions that, while not properly true of his being, help us understand how he will relate to us in terms of his purposes and will.

Indeed, Bavinck highlights the importance and graciousness of God dealing with us in this way: "If God were to speak to us in a divine language, not a creature would understand him. But what spells out his grace is the fact that from the moment of creation God stoops down to his creatures, speaking and appearing to them in human fashion."[6]

The Anthropomorphic Christ

The person of Christ, as the God-man, gives us the reason why God attributed to himself human parts and passions in the Old Testament. The Son related to the church in the Old Testament by dwelling in their midst (1 Cor. 10:4). And according to John Owen, in dwelling with the church, the Son

> constantly assumes unto himself human affections, to intimate that a season would come when he would immediately act in that nature. And, indeed, after the fall there is nothing spoken of God in the Old Testament, nothing of his institutions, nothing of the way and manner of dealing with the church, but what has respect unto the future incarnation of Christ.[7]

In other words, God attributes parts and passions to himself not only to help us more clearly understand his purposes toward his people but also to set the stage, so to speak, for the incarnation of the Son of God.

Owen makes this important point: "It had been absurd to bring in God under perpetual anthropopathies, as grieving, repenting, being angry, well pleased, and the like, were it not but that the divine person intended was to take on him the nature wherein such affections do dwell."[8]

Thus, everything anthropomorphically or improperly attributed to God, as if he had arms or grief, is actually properly attributed to Christ as the God-man. For example, the Son, according to his human nature, grieves (Mark 3:5). [What is impossible for God, who cannot change, is possible for Christ, because of the glory of the incarnation.] In him we are able to affirm both his divine unchangeability and his human ability to express passions. The Son of God, as one person with two natures, is both unchangeable and changeable; he experiences an infinite joy in his deity, but while on earth, he also experienced an inexpressible sorrow in his humanity.

God is anthropomorphic, but he condescends to us not simply that we may understand him but also that we may have a real hope of salvation. In Christ, we can see God; in Christ, we will one day see God's arms, eyes, face, and lips. Apart from Christ, however, all the biblical language of God's passions and parts are of no use to us.

Application

The early church father Gregory of Nazianzus famously said, "Whatever is not assumed is not healed/redeemed."[9] Our body-souls stand in need of redemption. Physically and spiritually, we are by nature unclean lepers in the eyes of God. We have turned aside to our own way. We are rebels and are maimed as such, with bodies that fail to function as God intended.

In this world, many try desperately to stop the rot of their physical degradation. Billions of dollars are spent each year in developed countries on enhancing physical beauty and seeking to ward off death by medical means. If this life is all we have, it makes sense that so many are consumed with how they look and how long they live. Their figure, stamina, heart, lungs, brain, skin, eyes, ears, nose, and lips are all in need of "help." But whether it is makeup or medicine, supplements or surgery, workouts or weight-watching, or whatever, we must avoid getting caught up in the world's obsession with the tangible things of this life. As

Christians, we ought not enslave ourselves to the vain principles of the world, which include a deep dissatisfaction with how we look or how long we live. In Christ, we possess abundant life and the hope of future resurrected life, when we shall look on God face-to-face, being like him who dared to be like us in every way.

God sent forth his Son in the likeness of sinful flesh. He prepared a body for him (Heb. 10:5). Christ's appearance during his time of humiliation was fitting for a man who was to be humiliated all the days of his earthly existence:

> For he grew up before him like a young plant,
>   and like a root out of dry ground;
> he had no form or majesty that we should look at him,
>   and no beauty that we should desire him. (Isa. 53:2)

As a true human being, Christ had a physical appearance on earth that lacked "beauty." Interesting questions have been raised about Christ's pre- and postresurrection physical appearance. While passages like Isaiah 53:2 may convince us that Jesus was not a beautiful person while on earth, many early church fathers (e.g., Tertullian, Origen, Ambrose, Chrysostom, and Augustine) argued otherwise, based on Psalm 45:2: "You are the most handsome of the sons of men; grace is poured upon your lips; therefore God has blessed you forever."

There is, I believe, an obvious difference between Christ's states of humiliation and exaltation, which would entail a change in his physical appearance. While his glory was veiled in his state of humiliation, the resurrection transformed his physical appearance in his exalted state to make him "the most handsome" of men.

As such, we can be confident that one day our physical beauty will change, and our mortality will put on immortality. Our glorious resurrection bodies will no longer carry the infirmities of this present age. But we shall also look a great deal better than we already do. This is why we do not need to become enslaved to the worldly obsessions with physical beauty and length of life.

God loves beauty and life, but he loves them both internally and externally. In heaven, both our inner beauty and life and our outer beauty and life shall harmonize perfectly. That is true for Christ now, and it will be true for us in the future.

Our passions will be perfectly guided by the Spirit because the Son of God took on human passions in order to impart to us these passions in their perfection. He took on hands and feet and arms and eyes in order that our hands and feet and arms and eyes would also be redeemed. But while we are being renewed inwardly day by day (2 Cor. 4:16), we have to wait for the outward renewal of our bodies (1 Cor. 15:42–49). In the life to come, bodies will differ in glory from one another, which is perhaps one reason why we should be more concerned about the inner self in this life.

That God became man in order to redeem man (body and soul) carries a host of practical implications for the Christian life, not least of which is the fact that we will possess beautiful body-souls for all eternity. Our body-soul relation, though not collapsing together, will be more intimate and harmonious and in greater communion with the life-giving Spirit. Thus, we put our hope in what awaits us more than in what this world can offer, which is, at best, a temporary beauty and life that ultimately becomes grotesque as we fade away.

EPILOGUE

I know that you can do all things,
 and that no purpose of yours can be thwarted.
"Who is this that hides counsel without
  knowledge?"
Therefore I have uttered what I did not understand,
 things too wonderful for me, which I did
  not know.
"Hear, and I will speak;
 I will question you, and you make it known
  to me."
I had heard of you by the hearing of the ear,
 but now my eye sees you;
therefore I despise myself,
 and repent in dust and ashes.

Job 42:2–6

"What are you, then, my God?" Augustine asks. He answers as follows:

> You are most high, excellent, most powerful, omnipotent, supremely merciful and supremely just, most hidden yet intimately present, infinitely beautiful and infinitely strong, steadfast yet elusive, unchanging yourself though you control the change in all things, never new, never old, renewing all things yet wearing

down the proud though they know it not; ever active, ever at rest, gathering while knowing no need, supporting and filling and guarding, creating and nurturing and perfecting, seeking although you lack nothing. You love without frenzy, you are jealous yet secure, you regret without sadness, you grow angry yet remain tranquil, you alter your works but never your plan; you take back what you find although you never lost it; you are never in need yet you rejoice in your gains, never avaricious yet you demand profits. You allow us to pay you more than you demand, and so you become our debtor, yet which of us possesses anything that does not already belong to you? You owe us nothing, yet you pay your debts; you write off our debts to you, yet you lose nothing thereby.

After saying all that, what have we said, my God, my life, my holy sweetness? What does anyone who speaks of you really say? Yet woe betide those who fail to speak, while the chatterboxes go on saying nothing.[1]

What do we really say when we speak of God? It is a wonder that we can say anything about him, and yet he commands us to do so and to do it truly and well.

So how well are we doing? Listen to the pastoral prayers in the church, if they are even offered up in public worship. So many of them lack the rich biblical vocabulary that does justice to the God of heaven and earth as he reveals himself in Scripture. Look at so many worship songs that speak in vain generalities of God. Compare them with the Psalms, composed by godly men who, as governed by the Spirit, could not say enough about the majestic God they loved.

J. I. Packer once mentioned to me what he thought was the most impressive feature of Martyn Lloyd-Jones's preaching: "He brought God into the pulpit." How many preachers today bring God into the pulpit? Are God's people aware of Isaiah's God?

To whom then will you liken God,
or what likeness compare with him?

An idol! A craftsman casts it,
    and a goldsmith overlays it with gold
    and casts for it silver chains.
He who is too impoverished for an offering
    chooses wood that will not rot;
he seeks out a skillful craftsman
    to set up an idol that will not move.

Do you not know? Do you not hear?
    Has it not been told you from the beginning?
    Have you not understood from the foundations of the earth?
It is he who sits above the circle of the earth,
    and its inhabitants are like grasshoppers;
who stretches out the heavens like a curtain,
    and spreads them like a tent to dwell in;
who brings princes to nothing,
    and makes the rulers of the earth as emptiness.
      (Isa. 40:18–23)

Where else does one find such language about God?

If we are really concerned to preach Christ crucified and resurrected, then surely we ought to couple such preaching with great descriptions of God. The person and work of Christ testifies to a God greater than that which can be conceived. In other words, a poor doctrine of God leads to a poor understanding of Christ, and vice versa.

It is to our great advantage to know God. "Fresh joys spring continually from his face," Thomas Watson declares; "he is as much to be desired after millions of years by glorified souls as at the first moment."[2]

Only God can perpetually satisfy in this life and that to come. God encounters us as infinite in goodness, knowledge, wisdom, blessedness, and so forth, and so can forever (and ever and ever) freshly supply us with himself. This he will do through his Son by the power of the Holy Spirit.

Anyone united to Christ by the power of the Spirit in this life has the privilege of remaining so in the life to come, when our happiness in the pursuit of God will forever grow. Indeed, Augustine rightly and wonderfully exclaimed, "How foolish are they who know not God! So many good things before their eyes, yet *Him Who Is* they fail to see."[3]

Amen.

ACKNOWLEDGMENTS

I am thankful to Bob McKelvey, Steve Tipton, Dolf Te Velde, Jonathan Tomes, David Carnes, and Garry Vanderveen for their help with this manuscript.

Conversations with Peter Escalante, Derek Rishmawy, Mark Garcia, Michael Lynch, Richard Muller, and G. A. van den Brink have also helped me in thinking through various issues related to the doctrine of God.

Justin Taylor spoke to me about writing a book for Crossway. I am grateful that he felt a book on God was needed. Crossway has been a pleasure to work with. David Barshinger's editorial work has been superb. Many others have also worked very hard to make this book a reality.

As always, I thank my congregation at Faith Vancouver Presbyterian Church for their encouragement and desire to see the wider kingdom helped through projects like this one.

My wife, Barb, and my children, Katie, Josh, Thomas, and Matthew, are all deserving of a special award for their patience when I am consumed at various times with my writing projects.

Finally, to the triune God, I pray that I have promoted the truth and not error in this book. To the degree that I have done that, I give all the glory and praise to my God, whom I love and serve.

NOTES

Preface
1. Thomas Watson, *Body of Divinity* (Edinburgh: Banner of Truth, 1970), 194.
2. Watson, *Body of Divinity*, 194.
3. Jonathan Edwards, "God Glorified in the Work of Redemption, by the Greatness of Man's Dependence upon Him, in the Whole of It (1731)," in *The Sermons of Jonathan Edwards: A Reader*, ed. Wilson H. Kimnach, Kenneth P. Minkema, and Douglas A. Sweeney (New Haven, CT: Yale University Press, 1999), 74–75.

Introduction
1. James Henley Thornwell, *The Collected Writings of James Henley Thornwell*, ed. John B. Adger (Richmond, VA: Presbyterian Committee of Publication, 1871), 1:107.
2. Charles H. Spurgeon, "The Immutability of God," in *The New Park Street Pulpit* (Pasadena, TX: Pilgrim Publications, 1975), 1:1.
3. Anselm of Canterbury, *Proslogion*, in *Anselm of Canterbury: The Major Works*, ed. Brian Davies and G. R. Evans, Oxford World's Classics (New York: Oxford University Press, 1998), 87.
4. Thomas Goodwin, *A Discourse of the Glory of the Gospel*, in *The Works of Thomas Goodwin* (Edinburgh: James Nichol, 1862), 4:267.

Chapter 1: God Is Triune
1. Gregory of Nazianzus, *Oration 40: On Holy Baptism*, in *Nicene and Post-Nicene Fathers*, 2nd series, ed. Philip Schaff and Henry Wace (New York: Christian Literature, 1893), 7:375.
2. John Owen, *A Brief Declaration and Vindication of the Doctrine of the Trinity*, in *The Works of John Owen*, vol. 2, *Communion with God*, ed. William H. Goold (1862; repr., Edinburgh: Banner of Truth, 1965), 378.
3. Owen, *Vindication of the Trinity*, in *Works*, 2:379.
4. Owen, *Vindication of the Trinity*, in *Works*, 2:379.
5. Owen, *Vindication of the Trinity*, in *Works*, 2:379.
6. Francis Cheynell, *The Divine Triunity of the Father, Son, and Holy Spirit* (London: T. R. and E. M. for S. Gellibrand, 1650), 42.

7. Thomas Goodwin, *The Objects and Acts of Justifying Faith*, in *The Works of Thomas Goodwin* (Edinburgh: James Nichol, 1864), 8:378–79.
8. Owen, *Of Communion with God the Father, Son, and Holy Ghost*, in *Works*, 2:33–34.
9. Owen, *Communion with God*, in *Works*, 2:32.
10. Owen, *Communion with God*, in *Works*, 2:262.

Chapter 2: God Is Simple

1. Augustine, *On the Trinity* 6.4.6, in *The Fathers of the Church*, vol. 45, *Saint Augustine: The Trinity*, trans. Stephen McKenna (Washington, DC: Catholic University of America Press, 1963), 205.
2. Irenaeus, *Against Heresies* 2.13.3, in *The Ante-Nicene Fathers*, vol. 1, *The Apostolic Fathers: Justin Martyr, Irenaeus* (New York: Charles Scribner's Sons, 1903), 374.
3. Stephen Charnock, *The Existence and Attributes of God*, in *The Works of Stephen Charnock* (1864; repr., Edinburgh: Banner of Truth, 2010), 2:124.
4. Thomas Boston, *An Illustration of the Doctrines of the Christian Religion, with Respect to Faith and Practice*, in *The Whole Works of the Late Reverend Thomas Boston of Ettrick* (Aberdeen: George and Robert King, 1848), 1:158.
5. This sentence is drawn from Joel R. Beeke and Mark Jones, *A Puritan Theology: Doctrine for Life* (Grand Rapids, MI: Reformation Heritage Books), 72. Used by permission of Reformation Heritage Books.
6. Thomas Goodwin, *Of Christ the Mediator*, in *The Works of Thomas Goodwin* (Edinburgh: James Nichol, 1863), 5:16.
7. A. W. Tozer, *The Attributes of God: A Journey into the Father's Heart* (Camp Hill, PA: Christian Publications, 1997), 71.
8. Jonathan Edwards, "Christian Graces Concatenated Together," sermon 12 of *Charity and Its Fruits*, in *The Works of Jonathan Edwards*, vol. 8, *Ethical Writings*, ed. Paul Ramsey (New Haven, CT: Yale University Press), 328, 330.

Chapter 3: God Is Spirit

1. "Immortal, Invisible, God Only Wise," by Walter C. Smith, first published in *Hymns of Christ and the Christian Life* (1867).

Chapter 4: God Is Infinite

1. Stephen Charnock, *The Existence and Attributes of God*, in *The Works of Stephen Charnock* (1864; repr., Edinburgh: Banner of Truth, 2010), 1:279.
2. Maximus the Confessor, *In Epistula Dionysii* 1, in Patrologia Graeca, ed. J.-P. Migne (Paris, 1857–1886), 4:529A.
3. John Flavel, *The Works of John Flavel* (1820; repr., Edinburgh: Banner of Truth, 1997), 3:147.
4. Herman Bavinck, *Reformed Dogmatics*, vol. 2, *God and Creation*, ed. John Bolt, trans. John Vriend (Grand Rapids, MI: Baker Academic, 2004), 160.

5. Thomas Goodwin, *Of Christ the Mediator*, in *The Works of Thomas Goodwin* (Edinburgh: James Nichol, 1863), 5:104.

6. Goodwin, *Of Christ the Mediator*, in *Works*, 5:119.

7. See Dolf te Velde, ed., *Synopsis Purioris Theologiae, Synopsis of a Purer Theology: Latin Text and English Translation*, vol. 1, *Disputations 1–23*, trans. Riemer A. Faber, Latin text ed. Rein Ferwerda (Leiden: Brill, 2014), 215, as the question is highly complicated and beyond the aims of this chapter.

8. Francis Turretin, *Institutes of Elenctic Theology*, ed. James T. Dennison Jr., trans. George Musgrave Giger (Phillipsburg, NJ: P&R, 1997), 2:328.

9. Goodwin, *Of Christ the Mediator*, in *Works*, 5:119.

10. Goodwin, *A Discourse of the Glory of the Gospel*, in *Works*, 4:267.

11. Matthew Mead, *The Almost Christian Discovered; or, the False Professor Tried and Cast* (London: William Baynes and Son, 1825), 241.

Chapter 5: God Is Eternal

1. Stephen Charnock, *The Existence and Attributes of God*, in *The Works of Stephen Charnock* (1864; repr., Edinburgh: Banner of Truth, 2010), 1:368.

2. Louis Berkhof, *Summary of Christian Doctrine* (Tigard, OR: Monergism Books, 2011), Kindle edition, chap. 6.

3. Charnock, *Existence and Attributes of God*, in *Works*, 1:349.

4. Anselm, *Monologion and Proslogion, with the Replies of Gaunilo and Anselm*, trans. Thomas Williams (Indianapolis: Hackett, 1996), 106.

5. This section is adapted from Mark Jones, "Hell's Horrors vs. Heaven's Happiness (Updated)," in cooperation with and first published by the Alliance of Confessing Evangelicals at *reformation21* (blog), May 4, 2015, http://www.reformation21.org/blog/2015/05/hells-horrors-vs-heavens-happi.php.

6. Thomas Goodwin, *Two Discourses* (London: J. D. for Jonathan Robinson, 1693), 195.

Chapter 6: God Is Unchangeable

1. Herman Bavinck, *Reformed Dogmatics*, vol. 2, *God and Creation*, ed. John Bolt, trans. John Vriend (Grand Rapids, MI: Baker Academic, 2004), 156.

2. Thomas Vincent, *A Family Instructional Guide* (1980; repr., Simpsonville, SC: Christian Classics Foundation, 1996), Logos ebook, 28.

3. Stephen Charnock, *The Existence and Attributes of God*, in *The Works of Stephen Charnock* (1864; repr., Edinburgh: Banner of Truth, 2010), 1:401.

4. Charnock, *Existence and Attributes of God*, in *Works*, 1:401.

5. Bavinck, *Reformed Dogmatics*, 2:143.

Chapter 7: God Is Independent

1. Herman Bavinck, *Reformed Dogmatics*, vol. 2, *God and Creation*, ed. John Bolt, trans. John Vriend (Grand Rapids, MI: Baker Academic, 2004), 152.

2. Anselm of Canterbury, *Proslogion*, in *Anselm of Canterbury: The Major Works*, ed. Brian Davies and G. R. Evans, Oxford World's Classics (New York: Oxford University Press, 1998), 17.

Chapter 8: God Is Omnipresent

1. Edward Leigh, *A Treatise of Divinity: Consisting of Three Bookes* (London: E. Griffin for William Lee, 1647), 2:36.
2. Stephen Charnock, *The Existence and Attributes of God*, in *The Works of Stephen Charnock* (1864; repr., Edinburgh: Banner of Truth, 2010), 1:423.
3. Charnock, *Existence and Attributes of God*, in *Works*, 1:424.
4. Charnock, *Existence and Attributes of God*, in *Works*, 1:423.
5. Herman Bavinck, *Reformed Dogmatics*, vol. 2, *God and Creation*, ed. John Bolt, trans. John Vriend (Grand Rapids, MI: Baker Academic, 2004), 169.
6. John Murray, *Principles of Conduct: Aspects of Biblical Ethics* (Grand Rapids, MI: Eerdmans, 1971), 236.

Chapter 9: God Is Omniscient

1. Stephen Charnock, *The Existence and Attributes of God*, in *The Works of Stephen Charnock* (1864; repr., Edinburgh: Banner of Truth, 2010), 1:466–67.
2. Herman Bavinck, *Reformed Dogmatics*, vol. 2, *God and Creation*, ed. John Bolt, trans. John Vriend (Grand Rapids, MI: Baker Academic, 2004), 196.
3. Greg Boyd, "Molinism and Open Theism, Part 2," *RelKnew* (blog), May 2014, http://reknew.org/2014/05/molinism-and-open-theism-part-ii/.
4. Gregory A. Boyd, *God of the Possible: A Biblical Introduction to the Open View of God* (Grand Rapids, MI: Baker, 2000), 58.

Chapter 10: God Is Omnipotent

1. Stephen Charnock, *The Existence and Attributes of God*, in *The Works of Stephen Charnock* (1864; repr., Edinburgh: Banner of Truth, 2010), 2:106.
2. Problematizing this distinction, nominalist theology tends to treat absolute power as becoming operational, while in earlier scholastic thought it was a merely conceptual and hypothetical notion, needed to prevent the unqualified identification of God's power with what it actually performs.

Chapter 12: God Is Blessed

1. Benedict Pictet, *Theologia Christiana Benedicti Picteti* (London: R. Baynes, 1820), 2.4.7. My translation.
2. Edward Leigh, *A Treatise of Divinity: Consisting of Three Bookes* (London: E. Griffin for William Lee, 1647), 2:200.
3. John Owen, *Meditations and Discourses on the Glory of Christ*, in *The Works of John Owen*, vol. 1, *The Glory of Christ*, ed. William H. Goold (1862; repr., Edinburgh: Banner of Truth, 1965), 325.

4. Owen, *Meditations*, in *Works*, 1:368.

5. C. H. Spurgeon, "The Parable of the Lost Sheep," in *The Metropolitan Tabernacle Pulpit* (Pasadena, CA: Pilgrim Publications, 1973), 30:525–26.

6. Owen, *Meditations*, in *Works*, 1:414.

7. George Swinnock, *The Blessed and Boundless God*, Puritan Treasures for Today (1672; repr., Grand Rapids, MI: Reformation Heritage Books, 2014), 167.

Chapter 13: God Is Glorious

1. Thomas Watson, *A Body of Practical Divinity* (London: Thomas Parkurst, 1692), 1.

2. Thomas Goodwin, *The Knowledge of God the Father, and His Son Jesus Christ*, in *The Works of Thomas Goodwin* (Edinburgh: James Nichol, 1862), 4:455.

3. Thomas Goodwin, *An Exposition of the Second Chapter of the Epistle to the Ephesians*, in *Works*, 2:118.

4. John Arrowsmith, *Theanthrōpos, or, God-man: Being an Exposition upon the First Eighteen Verses of the First Chapter of the Gospel according to St. John* (London: Humphrey Moseley and William Wilson, 1660), 236.

5. Thomas Goodwin, *The Heart of Christ in Heaven towards Sinners on Earth* (London: R. Dawlman, 1642), 98.

6. John Owen, *Meditations and Discourses on the Glory of Christ*, in *The Works of John Owen*, vol. 1, *The Glory of Christ*, ed. William H. Goold (1862; repr., Edinburgh: Banner of Truth, 1965), 366.

7. John Piper, *Let the Nations Be Glad!: The Supremacy of God in Missions*, 3rd ed. (Grand Rapids, MI: Baker Academic, 2010), 50.

Chapter 14: God Is Majestic

1. Stephen Charnock, *The Existence and Attributes of God*, in *The Works of Stephen Charnock* (1864; repr., Edinburgh: Banner of Truth, 2010), 2:408.

2. John Calvin, *Institutes of the Christian Religion*, ed. John T. McNeill, trans. Ford Lewis Battles, Library of Christian Classics (Philadelphia: Westminster, 1960), 1.2.3.

3. Anselm of Canterbury, *Proslogion*, in *Anselm of Canterbury: The Major Works*, ed. Brian Davies and G. R. Evans, Oxford World's Classics (New York: Oxford University Press, 1998), 17.

Chapter 15: God Is Sovereign

1. Francis Turretin, *Institutes of Elenctic Theology*, ed. James T. Dennison Jr., trans. George Musgrave Giger (Phillipsburg, NJ: P&R, 1997), 1:219.

2. See William Ames, *The Marrow of Theology*, trans. and ed. John D. Eusden (1968; repr., Grand Rapids, MI: Baker, 1997), 1.6.1, 2; 1.9.3, 6, 14, 15, 19, 21.

3. William Pemble, "A Treatise of the Providence of God," in *The Workes of that Learned Minister of Gods Holy Word, Mr. William Pemble* (London: Tho. Cotes for E. F., 1635), 271.

4. John Owen, *A Display of Arminianism*, in *The Works of John Owen*, vol. 10, *The Death of Christ*, ed. William H. Goold (1862; repr., Edinburgh: Banner of Truth, 1965), 31.

5. Dolf te Velde, ed., *Synopsis Purioris Theologiae, Synopsis of a Purer Theology: Latin Text and English Translation*, vol. 1, *Disputations 1–23*, trans. Riemer A. Faber, Latin text ed. Rein Ferwerda (Leiden: Brill, 2014), 263.

6. Obadiah Sedgwick, *Providence Handled Practically*, ed. Joel R. Beeke and Kelly Van Wyck (Grand Rapids, MI: Reformation Heritage Books, 2007), 9.

7. Velde, *Synopsis Purioris Theologiae*, 279.

8. Parts of this section are adapted from Mark Jones, "A Strangled Baby and a Gold Cup," in cooperation with and first published by the Alliance of Confessing Evangelicals at *reformation21* (blog), August 22, 2014, http://www.reformation21.org/blog/2014/08/a-strangled-baby-a-gold-cup.php.

9. Quoted in Willem J. van Asselt, Michael D. Bell, Gert van den Brink, Rein Ferwerda, eds., *Scholastic Discourse: Johannes Maccovius (1588–1644) on Theological and Philosophical Distinctions and Rules* (Apeldoorn: Instituut voor Reformatieonderzoek, 2009), 173.

Chapter 16: God Is Love

1. J. I. Packer, *Knowing God* (Downers Grove, IL: InterVarsity Press, 1973), 117.

2. Augustine, quoted in John Calvin, *Institutes of the Christian Religion*, ed. John T. McNeill, trans. Ford Lewis Battles, Library of Christian Classics (Philadelphia: Westminster, 1960), 2.16.4.

3. William Bates, *The Harmony of the Divine Attributes in the Contrivance and Accomplishment of Man's Redemption* (1853; repr., Birmingham, AL: Solid Ground Christian Books, 2010), 152.

4. Bates, *Harmony of the Divine Attributes*, 153.

5. Bates, *Harmony of the Divine Attributes*, 153.

6. John Love, *Discourses on Select Passages of the Scripture* (Edinburgh: Andrew Jack, 1829), 23.

Chapter 17: God Is Good

1. Herman Bavinck, *Reformed Dogmatics*, vol. 2, *God and Creation*, ed. John Bolt, trans. John Vriend (Grand Rapids, MI: Baker Academic, 2004), 210.

2. Stephen Charnock, *The Existence and Attributes of God*, in *The Works of Stephen Charnock* (1864; repr., Edinburgh: Banner of Truth, 2010), 2:285.

3. Charnock, *Existence and Attributes of God*, in *Works*, 2:290.

4. Charnock, *Existence and Attributes of God*, in *Works*, 2:290.

5. Charnock, *Existence and Attributes of God*, in *Works*, 2:315–16.

6. Charnock, *Existence and Attributes of God*, in *Works*, 2:318.

7. Charnock, *Existence and Attributes of God*, in *Works*, 2:319.

8. This section is adapted from Mark Jones, "More Goodness Shown to Us Than to Christ," in cooperation with and first published by the Alliance of Confessing Evangelicals at *reformation21* (blog), January 11, 2016, http://www.reformation21.org/blog/2016/01/god-loved-us-more -than-his-son.php.
9. John Owen, *The Death of Death in the Death of Christ*, in *The Works of John Owen*, vol. 10, *The Death of Christ*, ed. William H. Goold (1862; repr., Edinburgh: Banner of Truth, 1965), 285.
10. Charnock, *Existence and Attributes of God*, in *Works*, 2:322.
11. Charnock, *Existence and Attributes of God*, in *Works*, 2:322–23.
12. Benedict Pictet, *Theologia Christiana Benedicti Picteti* (London: R. Baynes, 1820), 318–19. My translation.

Chapter 18: God Is Patient
1. Edward Leigh, *Treatise of Divinity: Consisting of Three Bookes* (London: E. Griffin for William Lee, 1647), 2:99.
2. Stephen Charnock, *The Existence and Attributes of God*, in *The Works of Stephen Charnock* (1864; repr., Edinburgh: Banner of Truth, 2010), 2:504.
3. Charnock, *Existence and Attributes of God*, in *Works*, 2:506.
4. Charnock, *Existence and Attributes of God*, in *Works*, 2:518–19.
5. Leigh, *Treatise of Divinity*, 2:186.
6. Charnock, *Existence and Attributes of God*, in *Works*, 2:528.
7. Charnock, *Existence and Attributes of God*, in *Works*, 2:544.
8. Charnock, *Existence and Attributes of God*, in *Works*, 2:544.

Chapter 19: God Is Merciful
1. Thomas Goodwin, *An Exposition of the First Chapter of the Epistle to the Ephesians*, in *The Works of Thomas Goodwin* (Edinburgh: James Nichol, 1861), 1:144.
2. Thomas Watson, *Body of Divinity* (Edinburgh: Banner of Truth, 1974), 93.
3. Francis Turretin, *Institutes of Elenctic Theology*, ed. James T. Dennison Jr., trans. George Musgrave Giger (Phillipsburg, NJ: P&R, 1992), 1:12–13.
4. Thomas Brooks, *A Cabinet of Jewels*, in *The Works of Thomas Brooks*, ed. Alexander Balloch Grosart (Edinburgh: James Nichol, 1866), 3:272.
5. Thomas Goodwin, *A Discourse of the Glory of the Gospel*, in *Works*, 4:270.
6. John Owen, *An Exposition of the Epistle to the Hebrews*, ed. William H. Goold (1862; repr., Edinburgh: Banner of Truth, 1991), 3:469.
7. Owen, *Exposition of Hebrews*, 3:470.
8. Owen, *Exposition of Hebrews*, 3:485.
9. Watson, *Body of Divinity*, 99.
10. Thomas Watson, *The Beatitudes* (1660; repr., London: Banner of Truth, 1971), 151.

Chapter 20: God Is Wise

1. Edward Leigh, *Treatise of Divinity: Consisting of Three Bookes* (London: E. Griffin for William Lee, 1647), 2:65.
2. John Calvin, *Institutes of the Christian Religion*, ed. John T. McNeill, trans. Ford Lewis Battles, Library of Christian Classics (Philadelphia: Westminster, 1960), 1.5.2.
3. Portions of this section are adapted from Joel R. Beeke and Mark Jones, *A Puritan Theology: Doctrine for Life* (Grand Rapids, MI: Reformation Heritage Books), 72–73. Used by permission of Reformation Heritage Books.
4. John Owen, *Meditations and Discourses on the Glory of Christ*, in *The Works of John Owen*, vol. 1, *The Glory of Christ*, ed. William H. Goold (1862; repr., Edinburgh: Banner of Truth, 1965), 300.
5. John Owen, *An Exposition of the Epistle to the Hebrews*, ed. William H. Goold (1862; repr., Edinburgh: Banner of Truth, 1991), 3:30.
6. Owen, *Exposition of Hebrews*, 3:31.
7. Stephen Charnock, *The Existence and Attributes of God*, in *The Works of Stephen Charnock* (1864; repr., Edinburgh: Banner of Truth, 2010), 2:51.
8. Charnock, *Existence and Attributes of God*, in *Works*, 2:51.
9. Thomas Ridgley, *A Body of Divinity: . . . Being the Substance of Several Lectures on the Assembly's Larger Catechism* (New York: Robert Carter and Brothers, 1855), 73.

Chapter 21: God Is Holy

1. Edward Leigh, *Treatise of Divinity: Consisting of Three Bookes* (London: E. Griffin for William Lee, 1647), 2:189.
2. Stephen Charnock, *The Existence and Attributes of God*, in *The Works of Stephen Charnock* (1864; repr., Edinburgh: Banner of Truth, 2010), 2:194.
3. Charnock, *Existence and Attributes of God*, in *Works*, 2:194.
4. Leigh, *Treatise of Divinity*, 2:188.
5. Thomas Watson, *Body of Divinity* (Edinburgh: Banner of Truth, 1974), 83.
6. Charnock, *Existence and Attributes of God*, in *Works*, 2:192.
7. Charnock, *Existence and Attributes of God*, in *Works*, 2:197.
8. Charnock, *Existence and Attributes of God*, in *Works*, 2:198.
9. Charnock, *Existence and Attributes of God*, in *Works*, 2:198.
10. Portions of this section are adapted from Joel R. Beeke and Mark Jones, *A Puritan Theology: Doctrine for Life* (Grand Rapids, MI: Reformation Heritage Books), 76–77. Used by permission of Reformation Heritage Books.
11. Charnock, *Existence and Attributes of God*, in *Works*, 2:211.
12. Charnock, *Existence and Attributes of God*, in *Works*, 2:211.
13. Charnock, *Existence and Attributes of God*, in *Works*, 2:211.
14. John Owen, *A Discourse concerning the Holy Spirit*, in *The Works of John Owen*, vol. 3, *The Holy Spirit*, ed. William H. Goold (1862; repr., Edinburgh: Banner of Truth, 1965), 570.

15. Owen, *Discourse concerning the Holy Spirit*, in *Works*, 3:571.
16. Herman Bavinck, *Reformed Dogmatics*, vol. 4, *Holy Spirit, Church, and New Creation*, ed. John Bolt, trans. John Vriend (Grand Rapids, MI: Baker Academic, 2008), 248.
17. Bavinck, *Reformed Dogmatics*, 4:249.

Chapter 22: God Is Faithful

1. Thomas Goodwin, *Of Christ the Mediator*, in *The Works of Thomas Goodwin* (Edinburgh: James Nichol, 1861), 5:7.
2. Goodwin, *Of Christ the Mediator*, in *Works*, 5:28.
3. John Owen, *An Exposition of the Epistle to the Hebrews*, ed. William H. Goold (1862; repr., Edinburgh: Banner of Truth, 1991), 3:486.

Chapter 23: God Is Gracious

1. Edward Leigh, *Treatise of Divinity: Consisting of Three Bookes* (London: E. Griffin for William Lee, 1647), 2:175.
2. John Owen, *A Discourse concerning the Holy Spirit*, in *The Works of John Owen*, vol. 3, *The Holy Spirit*, ed. William H. Goold (1862; repr., Edinburgh: Banner of Truth, 1965), 168–69.
3. Thomas Goodwin, *The Work of the Holy Ghost in Our Salvation*, in *The Works of Thomas Goodwin* (Edinburgh: James Nichol, 1863), 6:54.
4. Goodwin, *The Work of the Holy Ghost in Our Salvation*, in *Works*, 6:55.
5. Francis Roberts, *The Mysterie and Marrow of the Bible: viz. God's Covenants with Man. . . .* (London: R. W. for George Calvert, 1657), 105.
6. This section is adapted from Mark Jones, "Can Humans Merit before God? (2 of 2)," in cooperation with and first published by the Alliance of Confessing Evangelicals at *reformation21* (blog), April 21, 2015, http://www.reformation21.org/blog/2015/04/can-humans-merit-before-god-2.php.
7. Owen, *Discourse concerning the Holy Spirit*, in *Works*, 3:168–69.
8. Herman Bavinck, *Reformed Dogmatics*, vol. 3, *Sin and Salvation in Christ*, ed. John Bolt, trans. John Vriend (Grand Rapids, MI: Baker Academic, 2006), 292.
9. C. H. Spurgeon, "A Testimony to Free and Sovereign Grace," in *The Complete Works of C. H. Spurgeon*, vol. 33 (Harrington, DE: Delmarva, 2013), sermon no. 1953.

Chapter 24: God Is Just

1. Edward Leigh, *Treatise of Divinity: Consisting of Three Bookes* (London: E. Griffin for William Lee, 1647), 2:181–82.
2. Francis Turretin, *Institutes of Elenctic Theology*, ed. James T. Dennison Jr., trans. George Musgrave Giger (Phillipsburg, NJ: P&R, 1997), 1:239.
3. Turretin, *Institutes*, 1:239.
4. Patrick Gillespie, *The Ark of the Covenant Opened: Or, A Treatise of the Covenant of Redemption between God and Christ as the Foundation of the Covenant of Grace* (London: Tho. Parkhurst, 1677), 40.

5. Quoted in Thomas Watson, *Body of Divinity* (Edinburgh: Banner of Truth, 1974), 90.
6. Watson, *Body of Divinity*, 90.
7. Watson, *Body of Divinity*, 92.

Chapter 25: God Is Angry

1. William Ames, *The Marrow of Theology*, trans. and ed. John D. Eusden (1968; repr., Grand Rapids, MI: Baker, 1997), 87.
2. Herman Bavinck, *Reformed Dogmatics*, vol. 2, *God and Creation*, ed. John Bolt, trans. John Vriend (Grand Rapids, MI: Baker Academic, 2004), 222–23.
3. Bavinck, *Reformed Dogmatics*, 2:223.
4. Thomas Goodwin, *A Discourse on the Glory of the Gospel*, in *The Works of Thomas Goodwin* (Edinburgh: James Nichol, 1862), 4:269.

Chapter 26: God Is Anthropomorphic

1. Richard A. Muller, *Post-Reformation Reformed Dogmatics: The Rise and Development of Reformed Orthodoxy, ca. 1520 to ca. 1725*, vol. 3, *The Divine Essence and Attributes* (Grand Rapids, MI: Baker Academic, 2003), 553.
2. Muller, *Post-Reformation Reformed Dogmatics*, 3:553.
3. John Owen, *On the Death of Christ*, in *The Works of John Owen*, vol. 10, *The Death of Christ*, ed. William H. Goold (1862; repr., Edinburgh: Banner of Truth, 1965), 451.
4. Quoted in Muller, *Post-Reformation Reformed Dogmatics*, 3:558.
5. Herman Bavinck, *Reformed Dogmatics*, vol. 1, *Prolegomena*, ed. John Bolt, trans. John Vriend (Grand Rapids, MI: Baker Academic, 2003), 99.
6. Bavinck, *Reformed Dogmatics*, 1:100.
7. John Owen, *Meditations and Discourses on the Glory of Christ*, in *Works*, vol. 1, *The Glory of Christ*, 350.
8. Owen, *Meditations and Discourses*, in *Works*, 1:350.
9. Gregory of Nazianzus, Epistle 101.7.32, in St. Gregory of Nazianzus, *On God and Christ: The Five Theological Orations and Two Letters to Cledonius*, trans. Lionel Wickham, Popular Patristics Series 23 (Crestwood, NY: St. Vladimir's Seminary Press, 2002), 155.

Epilogue

1. Augustine, *The Confessions*, trans. Maria Boulding, ed. John E. Rotelle, pt. 1, vol. 1 of *The Works of Saint Augustine* (Hyde Park, NY: New City Press, 1990), 4.4.
2. Thomas Watson, *Body of Divinity* (Edinburgh: Banner of Truth, 1974), 23.
3. Augustine, *Confessions*, 8.2. Italics original.

GENERAL INDEX

Abelard, 17
absolute power, 86–89
accommodation, 61, 205
Adam
  obedience for reward, 137
  received grace in the garden, 178–79
  sin of, 198
aeviternity, 54
affections of God, 127, 194, 202–3
Ambrose, 155, 208
Ames, William, 194
"Ancient of Days," 52
angels, 33–34, 63, 144
Anselm, 11, 17, 18
  on aseity of God, 66
  on eternality of God, 53
  on justice of God, 188
  on majesty of God, 115
anthropomorphisms, in Scripture, 61, 205–7
Anthropomorphites, 39
anthropopathisms, 193
Arminius, Jacob, 80
Arrowsmith, John, 105
aseity. See God, independence of
assurance, from immutability of God, 61
atonement, 46–47
attributes of God, 18–19
  consistency in, 32
  explain other attributes, 59
  perfection of, 45

Augustine, 8, 17, 74, 208, 211–12, 214
  on attributes and essence of God, 32
  on justice of God, 190
  on love of God, 130–31

baptism, naming in, 95
Barth, Karl, 8
Bates, William, 131
Bavinck, Herman
  on anthropomorphisms in Scripture, 205–6
  on aseity of God, 66
  on holiness of God, 168–69
  on human nature of Christ, 181
  on infinity of God, 44
  on omniscience of God, 78–79
  on presence of Christ, 74
  on unchangeability of God, 59, 63–64
  on wrath of God, 195
beauty, 208–9
  and holiness, 165
Berkhof, Louis, 52
Bernard of Clairvaux, 155
blessedness, 97–102
body and soul, 41, 208–9
Bolton, Samuel, 145–46
Bonaventure, 54
Boston, Thomas, 34
Boyd, Greg, 80–81
Bradwardine, Thomas, 123
Brooks, Thomas, 152–53

226

on providence, 119
on the Trinity, 23–24
on wisdom of the Son, 159
on wrath of Father on the Son, 138

Packer, J. I., 19, 127, 212
passion, 127, 202–3
pastoral prayers, 212
patience, 143–48
Pemble, William, 119
personal glory, 104, 107
"persons-appropriate" language, 23, 37, 46
Pharisees, 84
physical power, 111
Pictet, Benedict
on God as blessed, 98
on good works, 140
on repentance of God, 205
Pinnock, Clark, 80
Piper, John, 106
power, 85–86, 110–11
absolute and ordained, 86–89
to act for a right end, 158
practical atheism, 75
prayer, ordained to accomplish certain ends, 89
preaching, 139
predestination, 119, 129
prescience, 77
pride, 182
primary holiness, 164
providence, 118–20, 135
and suffering, 122–24
and wisdom, 159

redemption, 129, 138, 207–9
displays God's wisdom, 160
remunerative justice, 186–87
repentance, 61
proper and relative, 62
repletive presence, 72–73
retributive justice, 186–87
reverence and awe, 114

righteous anger, 197
Roberts, Francis, on grace, 179
Rutherford, Samuel, on death of Christ, 188

sanctification, 147
and holiness, 168–69
Scripture, as anthropomorphic, 205–7
Sedgewick, Obadiah, on providence, 120
self-sufficiency, 69
sin, primary object of God's displeasure, 165
Socinians, 179
Son. *See also* Jesus Christ
communion with, 27–28
deity of, 22
displays the attributes of God, 189
eternal generation of, 68
as Mediator, 160
as servant, 68
special object of Father's love, 130
as wisdom of God, 159–60
wrath of the Father poured on, 137–38
spatiality, 72
special mercy, 151–52
Spurgeon, Charles, 16–17
on grace of God, 182
on joy of Christ, 100
steadfast love, 63, 172
suffering, and justice of God, 190
"superabounding" grace, 179–80
superadded gift, 179
superadded glory, 105
Swinnock, George, 101
Synopsis of Purer Theology (1625), 119–21

Tertullian, 208
theophanies, 39
Thomas Aquinas, 17

Thornwell, James Henley, 15–16
time, 52–56
Tozer, A. W., 34–35
transcendent holiness, 165
treasured possession, 133
trials and tribulations, faithfulness
    in, 176
Trinity, 21–29
  love within, 128
Turretin, Francis, 46
  on death of Christ, 189
  on mercy of God, 151
  on will of God, 118
Twisse, William, 188

union with Christ, 49, 74, 213

Vincent, Thomas, 60
vision of God, 38–40

Watson, Thomas, 11–12
  on glory of God, 103
  on holiness of God, 164–65
  on justice of God, 190, 191
  on knowing God, 213
  on mercy of God, 150, 155

way of affirmation, 37–38
way of negation, 38
Weinandy, Thomas, 18
Westminster Confession of Faith
  on communication of properties,
    46–47
  on God, 38
  on God's fatherly displeasure,
    195–96
  on good and necessary conse-
    quence, 24
  on good works, 140
  on impassibility of God, 202
  on the Trinity, 24–25
will of God, 117–19
  and evil, 121
  independence of, 117
  outward, 194
  simplicity of, 118
  as single, 22–23
wisdom, 157–61, 190
worship, 12, 41–42
worship songs, 212
wrath of God, 193–99

Yahweh, 91–95

SCRIPTURE INDEX

Scripture Index